The SECRETS of
Faith
INFERTILITY

The SECRETS of

Faith

INFERTILITY

An Untold Journey of Faith, Fertility, and Favor

DR. LATAZIA STUART

Unless otherwise noted, names of people and places have been altered to protect their privacy. This book is sold with the understanding that neither the author nor publisher is engaged in rendering medical, legal, or other professional advice. If medical, legal, or other expert assistance is required, the services of a competent professional should be sought.

Scripture quotations marked MSG are taken from *The Message*, copyright © 1993, 2002, 2018 by Eugene H. Peterson. Used by permission of NavyPress. All rights reserved. Represented by Tyndale House Publishers.

Scripture quotations marked (NIV) are taken from the Holy Bible, New International Version®, NIV.®Copyright © 1973, 1978, 1984, 2011 by Biblica, Inc.® Used by permission of Zondervan. All rights reserved worldwide. www.zondervan.com The "NIV" and "New International Version" are trademarks registered in the United States Patent and Trademark Office by Biblica, Inc.®

For permission requests, write to the publisher at milartpublishing@gmail.com.

Ordering Information:
Orders by U.S. trade bookstores and wholesalers. Quantity sales. Special discounts are available on quantity purchases by corporations, associations, and others. For special bulk order pricing use contact form at www.DoctorTazz.com.

Connect with Dr. Latazia Stuart:

Instagram: @DoctorTazz
Website: www.DoctorTazz.com
Email: Tazz@DoctorTazz.com

Cover photo credit: i4Perfection Photography

ISBN: 978-0-578-29834-4

AUTHOR BIO

Dr. Latazia Stuart (Tazz) is a Christian mom of three young kids who is passionate about supporting women and couples experiencing infertility, miscarriage, and infant loss.

Through her personal journey, Tazz has learned how to maximize her faith in challenging life seasons and use her faith in God to build hope and bring joy, helping those she meets experience peace.

Tazz is a wife, mom, speaker, author, university dean, children's ministry leader, and mentor to young business leaders. Her creative energy is seen while wearing many hats and in her passion to serve God through her service to others. She has island roots from The Bahamas, and currently resides in Central Florida with her husband and kids. Dr. Tazz's personal mission is to build hope and bring joy!

Connect with Dr. Tazz:
Instagram - @DoctorTazz
Website - Doctortazz.com

DEDICATION

This book is dedicated to all mothers and fathers in waiting who are in need of hope to find joy in the gift of life to come.

This book is also dedicated to the memory of my babies DJ, Azaria, and Angel, and all the sleeping babies who left the path open for mothers in waiting to welcome a future new gift of life.

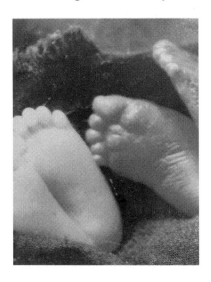

DJ & Azaria Stuart - January 2009.

FOREWORD

Faith can seem like an abstract concept if it's limited to just a few lines in scripture or heroic stories in literature. But what is faith, really? This invisible, yet dynamic source of strength is powerful enough to cause you to rise above tragedy and soar peacefully over crises. Where does it come from? Can anyone access it? Or is it just reserved for the "perfect Christians"? Every now and then, God will provide the answers to such questions by allowing you the privilege of sitting in the front row seat of a human drama being enacted on the stage of life. In living color, you get to witness persistent faith amidst painful failure - all testifying to the glory of a powerful Father!!

My questions about faith were answered in the gift of this young life I adopted as she began her college journey - a journey of faith. How would she make it on her own in a different country? How would her bills be paid? Would she be able to create a new support system? These were my questions - not hers! She was absolutely convinced that, "With God all things are possible." From that point forward, I watched this young student blossom through one trial after another, one success after another, building a strong foundation of faith in the process. The repeated blows of personal loss could have easily overwhelmed and destroyed the average person, but with each strike the enemy inflicted, I've seen her faith rise higher!

I can only marvel and praise God for allowing me the opportunity to participate in Tazz's faith hike - yes it's been a hike - not a walk! One in which I was encouraged to inhale deeply the breath of God to keep climbing with her, even though there was no evidence of prayer being answered. The ultimate challenge came one day when she decided to make a surprise trip from FL to MD to deliver at my doorstep a baby blanket for us to pray over until God answered her prayer for a child to be born from her womb! Every day thereafter I would intercede for her - pleading that God would be gracious in giving her the desire of her heart - motherhood! It was her determined faith that bolstered my "help thou my unbelief" faith as, together, we waited patiently and expectantly for a positive response! In the fullness of time, just as Jesus pronounced in Scripture: *"Daughter your faith has made you whole,"* Tazz repeatedly received similar confirmations:

Daughter, your faith will allow you to bear not just one, but three children.

Daughter, your faith will sustain you even when it seemed like your children would be without their Dad.

Daughter, your faith will preserve you as you navigate the challenging roles of motherhood and career - providing promotions despite problems.

Daughter, your faith will ensure you can do all things through Christ - even completing an Ed.D. doctoral degree with His help!

And the story goes on and on, as I silently pray a sincere thank you to God for allowing me to see true faith in action in every step of Tazz's life hike! She has been a source of encouragement in dealing with my own struggles. Today, I guarantee you if you read this book to the end you would gain more than just the rehearsal of another interesting story. Reading this, you will experience a faith invitation for your own life - a challenge to live daily with faith-filled expectation as you learn to patiently wait on God!

In Him,

Brenda Billingy
Retired Pastor & Associate Ministerial Director,
Seventh-day Adventist Church,
North American Division

PREFACE

 Now faith is the confidence in what we hope for and assurance about what we do not see,"

Hebrews 11:1 (NIV).

Through this journey, I've come to learn that God loves to respond to faith. Sometimes He does this through the delivery of a delayed promise as He did for me. Not delayed by His standards, but by ours, because God never delays what He has purposefully timed for a specific point in our lives.

While we wait for His promise to be delivered, God desires for us to stay IN Him during our journey. I've learned that when we do this despite the inadequacies we may be experiencing, through Christ we can grow *INfaith*, *INfertility*, and prepare to be *INfavor* with God.

TABLE OF CONTENTS

PROLOGUE

For many years the enemy held me captive with fear, shame, and embarrassment. During this time, God never let me go and constantly whispered, *"I am with you always,"* (Matthew 28:20 NIV). Through my unexpected infertility journey that was riddled with needles, biopsies, miscarriages, marital challenges, and much more, I was barely clinging onto the roller coaster that took me over loops of faith, favor, and fertility. As I secretly got on this ride, many times I questioned whether my life, my actions, and my faith aligned with God's will.

The reality is infertility was never discussed in my church, my family, or my vibrant island community, and I felt painfully isolated.

There were the private moments when I comforted a mom in the neonatal intensive care unit (NICU) while a doctor told her there was nothing else they could do to save her three-day-old son she had delivered prematurely. There were moments of consoling a mother who gave birth to her stillborn daughter after eight months of pregnancy. And yet, another moment when I supported a couple trying to understand how to navigate the challenges of infertility. Each moment highlighted a common denominator, the secret of their infertility, and the need to pursue their faith, find fertility, and experience favor!

This book will boldly expose how the enemy's plan to discourage and crush my faith was conquered through *Faith INfertility*! It is my desire that this book will bring awareness to the secret struggles of infertility intersected with faith to create support for this social issue.

It is also my aspiration that this book will serve as a light to build hope and bring joy to the hearts of mothers in waiting, knowing God has not forgotten you!

It's time to activate *Faith INfertility*, unveil the secrets, build hope, and bring joy!!

INTRODUCTION

I never told anyone about the infertility challenges I was facing, not even my mother because honestly, I was embarrassed. I serve God, I'm a good person, and I give my all to my family, friends, and work colleagues. I did my very best to honor God with my time through personal time with Him and through service to others. And yes, I'm a woman! It may be an unconscious assumption, but I knew and believed I was designed and created by God Himself to procreate!

Are you living in a season of infertility and secrecy for fear that it shows a lack of faith in God? Have you experienced the loss of a precious baby prematurely and then questioned where God is? Have you and your friends and church family fervently prayed for your womb to carry a child to term? But yet, they don't know of the need to pray for your ability to even just conceive? Has your faith wavered with questions of whether your pursuit of fertility treatment was in alignment with God's will? Has your church missed the mark of acknowledging that infertility is a family and social issue that is prevalent, even in the church? We talk about many things, but we don't talk about infertility. In my entire life, I've never once heard the discussion of infertility shared in the church, within my family, or without a negative connotation within my Caribbean community.

My purpose for writing this book is to encourage and share with couples who have lived or are living this private struggle in silence. I want them to know that God is with them in this process and that they are not alone. There is no need to hide! I have learned through the years that this deep secret pain is one that many couples live with. They struggle to conceive, experience miscarriage(s), infant loss, and are embarrassed to share or seek help for an unexpected journey they never signed up for.

In this book, I will share answers to questions based on my experiences of secretly carrying pain and shame. I will now unveil my personal faith journey of infertility, miscarriages, misconceptions, and common fears that attempted to choke my faith in God. Despite my painful reality and my perceptions I now share how God restored my *Faith INfertility*.

The unfortunate reality is that many others may have experienced challenges with infertility or miscarriage. But like me, they are embarrassed to share it because of how their faith in God may be viewed by others. However, God wants me to share what I know based on my experience and what His word placed in my heart. It is my hope that it will uplift others on this journey to know they are not alone, and to identify God's purpose for their wait through their personal experience.

> *"And then God answered: 'Write this. Write what you see. Write it out in big block letters so that it can be read on the run. This vision-message is a witness pointing to what's coming. It aches for the coming—it can hardly wait! And it doesn't lie. If it seems slow in coming, wait. It's on its way. It will come right on time,'" Habakkuk 2:2-3 (MSG).*

Chapter 1

IT HAPPENED AGAIN

" *... and provide for those who grieve in Zion— to bestow on them a crown of beauty instead of ashes, the oil of joy instead of mourning, and a garment of praise instead of a spirit of despair. They will be called oaks of righteousness, a planting of the Lord for the display of his splendor,*" **Isaiah 61:3 (NIV)**.

It was a Friday morning and I was reaching out to Jana, my colleague in another state, to check in on a mutual colleague, Nina. Nina and Jana worked in the same office, and I wanted to know how Nina was doing as she was more than eight months pregnant and someone had sent me a note that her scheduled office baby shower had been canceled. I naturally assumed that Nina had delivered her baby early. Then, I heard Jana's voice drop on the other end of the phone as she sadly broke the news that Nina's baby had died, and that Nina had to deliver the baby as a stillborn. I was shocked! She was only two or three weeks away from giving birth to her beautiful baby daughter. There was so much excitement shared in our last conversation regarding the plans for her first child.

Halfway through my conversation with Jana and in the middle of a sentence as I was speaking, I choked. Out of nowhere, I suddenly choked up. I became overwhelmed and emotional. Then, I began uncontrollably crying. I was unable to speak and could not stop crying.

Jana sat silently on the phone line as my crying slowed and then she said with a whisper, "it's okay." I imagined she sensed I was grieving for Nina. Then I just blurted out, "No! No! It's not okay, this just happened last week. Last week my sister-in-law lost her baby too!" The reality was, my emotions were compounded as this was my sister-in-law's first child, and she miscarried on Mother's Day (that Mother's Day also happened to be my birthday).

My sister-in-law was at the end of her first trimester when her baby died. Until that moment, I had not talked about my sister-in-law's loss or felt any sense of grief. Sadly, I had not even spoken with her. Secretly, I was unclear as to whether I was giving her space, putting up a block to protect my feelings, or just did not have enough emotional time to process this. My sister-in-law and I were very close and she had become like my younger sister. She lived with me and her brother (my husband) for several years immediately following her finishing college. I was with her during her last ultrasound appointment and had deeply fallen in love with my precious niece (or nephew) who had a strong and beautiful heartbeat on the Doppler ultrasound. I had seen the beautiful head, arms, and legs moving around inside of her, and this little life had already stolen a part of my heart.

Until this moment, I had not grieved the loss of my niece or nephew. Although a week had passed, I was still processing why I could not bring myself to speak with my sister-in-law about this. I had put up a block! Yes, I felt guilty for not having called her, that's what I'm supposed to do right? I am typically always the first one to be there whenever a crisis hits. I am the one with the perfect solution to help my family through whatever we are facing. It's what I do personally and professionally, all the time. However, there I was at a loss for words and embarrassingly crying with a colleague I had never met. A colleague who lived many miles away, with whom I had only shared a remote professional working relationship. Was I crying for my colleague Nina, mourning for my sister-in-law, or were these tears for something else, something more? Jana was silent, it was awkward, I apologized.

Even though I barely knew Jana, and we only had a remote working relationship, I sensed she could tell I was overwhelmed with emotions and sympathized with me. Little did she realize I knew the exact pain of having experienced the loss of my own three precious babies on a roller coaster infertility journey. The foundation of my faith was shaken in secret. Due to my infertility struggles, and my baby losses my faith was almost broken, but God! This story is my journey of faith, fertility, and favor on the road to *Faith INfertility*.

As you read this, know that the time is now to **remain steadfast** *INfaith INfertility* **and prepare to be** *INfavor* **with God as He alone defines the destiny of your womb and the path to parenthood that He will design just for you.**

> *"And then God answered: Write this. Write what you see. Write it out in big block letters so that it can be read on the run. This vision-message is a witness pointing to what's coming. It aches for the coming – it can hardly wait! And it doesn't lie. If it seems slow in coming, wait. It's on its way. It will come right on time," Habakkuk 2:2-3 (MSG).*

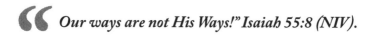

Chapter 2

YOU ARE NOT ALONE

" *Our ways are not His Ways!" Isaiah 55:8 (NIV).*

Privately, a few individuals (including family) knowing my history of pregnancy losses and likely suspecting our use of fertility treatment, reached out to me with questions and prayer requests for their fertility journey. Through those conversations and my personal experiences, I've come to realize that the journey of infertility is usually a lonely one that catches most couples by surprise and throws them off guard. One word comes to mind: unprepared, most couples are just unprepared. What young woman doesn't expect that when she gets pregnant she won't have her babies?

Some folks knew just parts of my story, my church family, close relatives, some of my dear friends, and a few former colleagues. Some were there to cheer me on with excitement when I first became pregnant. Several received holiday greeting cards announcing we were pregnant with twins. Another friend was there when my water broke and I miscarried during a work trip to Ohio. That was one of the most painful parts of my story. There was my church family who had care packages waiting when I returned to Florida. They prepared food for me because my babies died, and I was returning home with their ashes. There were the colleagues who attended the memorial service for my babies, the ones who knew of my work trip that cold winter in Ohio. Those were the ones who knew parts of my story.

Next, there were even fewer who knew this wasn't my only painful loss. Then, there are those who know another beautiful chapter which is the beauty of my three amazing, gifted children that show God's goodness in my life.

But my full story includes a very long painful private journey that existed during the first 10 years of my marriage. A private pain that many don't know, and I never envisioned, when I walked down the aisle to marry my best friend. This difficult deep secret journey that my husband and I carried alone and held for years, long before the first pregnancy loss.

From the moment we were married annoying comments or questions swirled around our journey to parenthood:
"Don't take too long to have babies."
"When are you going to have a child?"
"Is he shooting blanks?"
"Please try to have your first kid before you turn 30."
"You aren't barren are you?"

It was November 2001, just six months after having married my high school friend and now forever best friend. I was diagnosed with having several ovarian cysts that required surgical removal. Had it not been for the pain that I was experiencing I may have opted against having the surgery. The gynecologist performing the surgery had shared with me that the procedure was fairly common and that with the cysts being removed, my fertility would remain intact. I was not trying to get pregnant immediately as I was only 24 years old. My husband and I were having fun, and he was still in university. But as a newlywed, maintaining my fertility was still a priority.

We were married for only a few months when I began to experience pain in my abdomen. Initially, I ignored it and assumed it was likely only gas pain as I had developed poor eating habits around my new college teaching schedule. As the pain persisted, I began to identify the pattern of the pain becoming more intense during and immediately after my monthly menstrual cycle. I knew something was up. I went to my primary care physician who scheduled me to have an ultrasound where several cysts were located on my ovaries. He referred me to a gynecologist for additional follow up. I had experienced having a cyst in college and remember being prescribed some pills that allowed the cyst to break up during my monthly cycle. While I hoped this would be the same situation, something deep inside let me know it was probably not that simple given I was being referred to another doctor.

Without hesitation, I recall the gynecologist letting me know that the cysts I had on my ovaries were too big for pills to do the job and surgery would be required for them to be removed. Surgery on my ovaries? I wondered if there was no other option. He warned me that if the cysts were not removed it could create not just more pain but damage to my ovaries. So there I was 24 and a newlywed, facing surgery on my eggs (yes, my ovaries).

I never tolerated physical pain well and reflecting on how I was popping multiple painkillers to relieve the intensifying pain I was experiencing with each passing month, I agreed to the surgery. I was nervous as this would be my first ever surgery. I had grown up in an environment where no one ever wants to get "cut" (the island term for being operated on). I remember an aunt having had surgery for something and her post-op pain and recovery were horrible. I recall as a kid, hearing my mom share how she thanked God she had never had to get cut. Yet, here I was now agreeing to do exactly that. But what else could I do? I wanted to have my ovaries stay healthy and I wanted to get rid of the pain.

The doctor reassured me that the procedure was fairly simple and I should be able to go home within 24 hours after my surgery. He also reminded me that the procedure was appropriate if I wanted to have kids in the future. I recall specifically he didn't say it with any great urgency. Of course, I wanted to have kids in the future! Women are created to procreate, right? I wanted to make my husband a father someday and while it was not overtly expressed, I knew my parents looked forward to becoming grandparents of my children someday.

The surgery was scheduled for November 2001, about one week before the Thanksgiving holiday. It would be our first Thanksgiving as a married couple, and I would likely be in recovery mode. I was feeling comfortable and at peace that I was making the right decision to go ahead with the surgery. The surgery was scheduled at that time to allow for a substitute teacher to only be assigned for one week for my students, given that the Thanksgiving holiday was the following week. That would've given me a solid two-week recovery if it would be needed. Although the doctor said I would only need one week, my mom said to plan for two. Moms are usually right and this time she definitely was.

I have a variety of memories surrounding that surgical experience. My unconsciousness and pain-medicated brain started waking up, with foggy memory clips of surgery day in my head. I remember being wheeled into an elevator, coming in and out of consciousness, and I remembered being relieved that it was over, while simultaneously wondering whether my womb was okay. After successful surgical removal of the cysts, at my first follow-up appointment, I clearly recall the doctor saying, "Don't take too long to have kids." In fact, he was recommending that I have children within the next year. Today that mental note sticks with me; but, at the time, that timeline did not sit well with me and my husband as he was currently enrolled at a university in South Florida. We were newlyweds and having a baby at that time was just not in our plans. We wanted to enjoy just being with each other, finishing school, having fun, and traveling, so we waited. The doctor never stated it with critical urgency, but he did state it. At that time, I wondered if he thought I was from my parents' generation, who were eager to have kids as soon as they were married. Now I wonder, did he realize something during surgery related to my fertility?

We were 24 and 26, my husband had another year and a half to finish his university degree. I had just begun my college teaching career; we were looking forward to traveling together and hanging out with other young couples who had gotten married that year. We were living in a one-bedroom apartment, we had a student loan, and we were just getting adjusted to living on our own and managing our expenses as a young couple. We had to wait to have kids! We were in no way ready to become parents now. We wanted to someday, but just not now. The time was not right.

After the surgery, my husband and I went on with our life plans. He continued his studies and I carried on smartly in my new career teaching college classes. Life was simple, fun, and easy. We were very compatible with each other having been best friends for 9 years before getting married. Yes, we had our typical newlywed challenges: who cooked better meals, differences in how we folded towels, dividing household chores. We debated about who was responsible for putting the groceries away or loading the dishwasher. We were active in our local church which was only a few minutes from our home, and we both enjoyed singing in our church's young adult choir. I led a children's sign language group and had fun watching them grow and play around with each other. We enjoyed having lunch with friends after church service in their homes and also playing host to our own dinner parties. We enjoyed having kids around and my younger sister and cousin would come and spend summers with us each year.

Our enjoyment of life during that season with others especially children, let us know that we would be great parents someday. We just knew it! We never believed that we would encounter any roadblock on our journey to become parents. There was never any doubt in our minds, we both came from very fertile families. My husband was the oldest of five siblings and had many cousins. I had my siblings and many, many, many cousins. With the exception of one aunt, all my other aunts and uncles had multiple children.

Hubby graduated. We traveled throughout the U.S. and Europe, had lots of fun, and fully enjoyed the youthful stage of our married life. After my husband graduated and we purchased our first townhome, I felt IT - the itch to have a baby! As we had done at the beginning of each new year, we wrote down our plans to accomplish and it went something like this:

1. February, enjoy Valentine's Day.
2. March, travel to Europe and have fun trying to have a baby.
3. April, confirm pregnancy.
4. May, have a baby announcement party.
5. June, start remodeling room for baby.

Having only a few months prior, moved into a brand-new townhome with three bedrooms, the timing of everything seemed just perfect to have a child now. The time was perfect and my biological clock was ready and ticking before the big 3-0 arrived. That was the number I was targeting between 28 and 29 and definitely before I turn 30. But it did not happen.

I remember having purchased several ovulation test kits each month just to make sure we were having "fun" at the right time. I was tracking dates on the calendar as a backup. I became very in tune with what my body was doing. As time went by, within several months I began reading more books and checking out websites on 'how' to have a baby. Best positions, best foods, but eventually I started looking at what could be preventing me from having a baby. What problems we may be having, followed by what do we need to do or who do we need to see if this is a problem that we need to fix. I was not worried, but I did have a healthy concern about why I was not getting pregnant. I began to think about whether our decision to wait was truly worth all the reasons I had given. With each passing month of my menstrual cycle showing up, I thought more about the surgery and what the doctor had told me about not waiting too long to have kids.

Did we miss our opportunity? Surely the God we serve already has a solution for this and He will get us to the right person to figure this out. Did we know this was just the beginning of a 7-year challenge of strengthening our *Faith INfertility*? How could we? Did we share with anyone else what we were experiencing? Of course not! But, why not?

Chapter 3

HOSTAGE TO SECRETS OF INFERTILITY

"" *Have you hidden behind the 'perceived' shame that you have not conceived yet, while others around you are having babies? Have you wondered what they thought? Are you hiding in plain sight? Are you hiding behind a smile at the inquisitive comments from friends and family?*

I was in my 20s, surely having a baby would be no problem and surely it will happen before I was 30. I had the ultimate plan; I finish school, my husband would finish school, nice job, nice home, a baby, and we will live happily ever after. That's what everyone says should happen, that's the way it looks for most of my friends and other family members. Besides, when we got married an African pastor prayed during our wedding service that our house would be overflowing with children! The laughter within the church during that wedding day prayer was clear and audible. Certainly, God heard that prayer ring at the alter that Summer 2001.

So let's be honest, full transparency. When I was planning to have a baby, after two months nothing happened. So I began to explore readings or pictures that would let me know when the best time is to have a baby. I was excited, I was anxious, I was ready. After about 2 months of trying the calendar method, reinforcements were called in; to get more specific, that reinforcement was when I went out and purchased ovulation kits. After six months of trying, I had an elevated healthy concern about why it had not happened as yet. Months started to go by and I had purchased many ovulation kits to make sure we were doing it at the right time. But each month, nothing happened. Then I got to a place where I started buying dollar store pregnancy tests to confirm if pregnancy had occurred, even after seeing my period. I had read many times where women had seen their period but were still pregnant. I just really wanted to be pregnant. I wanted to be a mom. I wanted to give my husband a child. I wanted to live the storybook life as a cool, young, chic mom.

I had recently been promoted to a director role at my college and everything was going great. I was sure it was just a matter of time before I would be pregnant and holding a precious baby of my own to complete my pretty awesome life.

And then it happened, all within the span of a few months some of my church friends were pregnant at the same time. It felt like every week another friend shared that they were pregnant or a baby bump started to show. It was like four friends all at one time. And yes, I secretly prayed that I would be number five to join the crew. Time went on, baby showers were held, and coincidently, they all gave birth to beautiful baby girls. These precious baby girls were the dolls of the church. Four of them in a row, all cute adorable little princesses. Even though I never got pregnant during that time, I was still very excited for my friends. Frequently I thought to myself that any minute I would be pregnant, and my baby someday would be friends with their kids. The age difference between them I thought would be pretty small and they would still connect and be great friends. But there I was week after week, month after month, and yes year after year, still on bended knees at each prayer altar call during our church service, quietly praying, "Lord, please, please remember me."

It had almost been a year trying when I decided to research a specialist to get checked out. Could this be something more, and did we need help? I was never one to be afraid of going to the doctor, but I did become nervous as to what this process would look like for us trying to become pregnant. Then the process began, the 100+ questionnaire, the bloodwork, the scans, even one for my husband's sperm count check. And guess what?! Everything came back fine, including my husband's million swimmers. So what could the problem be? Why were we not getting pregnant?

The sequence of events that followed after these initial test results are not fully clear in my memory bank as I share this. However, I do recall the specialist eventually scheduling me for an outpatient laparoscopic procedure at a hospital that was about an hour away from my home. He said the only way to check everything was for me to go under anesthesia for a laparoscopic check of my ovaries and uterus. The time and distance did not matter as I was anxious to get to the reason as to what could be hindering our ability to have a child. And so we scheduled the procedure.

This time I was a bit nervous, but eager to know what was happening inside my body. Upon waking up from the procedure, the doctor advised that I had significant scar tissue wrapped around my ovaries. He said the scar tissue was everywhere and that was likely due to the surgery I had during my first year of marriage. While he expressed that he attempted to remove some of the scar tissue around my ovaries, he shared that he did not want to risk getting too much or too close to my ovaries to damage them as that would further limit my ability to have a child. He then shared his heart sinking recommendation. If I wanted to have a child, I would not be able to do so without fertility treatment. Specifically, he said I would need to explore the fertility treatment of in-vitro fertilization (IVF) because the scar tissues surrounding my ovaries blocked my eggs from being released into my tubes. In the back of my head, all I could think about was what did all of this mean? Was I infertile if my only course of action was fertility treatment?

The spiritual warrior within me began to cling to my faith. Of course, I would be able to have a child without assistance, my God can do anything! As my mind wandered, I thought the doctor probably suggested IVF because it was an expensive option and his office stood to gain a lot of money if I went that route. My spiritual indignation roared inside of me, "Hmph the devil is a liar!"

I recall the first time I went to the doctor to explore the option of fertility treatment. At that time it averaged around $10-$12,000. I recalled that my insurance plan did not include IVF treatment plans or the pre-work-up related to receiving future fertility treatment.

I didn't have money for IVF, and so clearly that's not the route I would have to go to have a child. Months continued to go by, and more family members and friends continue to have babies. And there I was with a nice job, an amazing husband, a beautiful home, great career, and no baby. Don't get me wrong, I was extraordinarily grateful for all my blessings of a 'good life' and everything else that God had given me in my life.

The unfortunate reality we must genuinely admit is that very often we are guilted by our feelings that our blessings should cover the pain of our losses or grief. On this journey, the reality is that good and great things in our life do not minimize any pain or challenges that we face. Our blessings should **never** be quantified against our difficulties. Life blessings and goodness should not be measured in comparison to minimize the challenges or sorrows we may face. The fact remains that I still wanted to become a mom. I wanted to make my husband a father, and give my parents the joy of being grandparents to my child. And yes, I was still grateful for all God's blessings in my life. Although a life oxymoron, gratitude and sorrow coexisted in my heart.

There were many days I would rationalize with God as to why he should give me a baby. I would rationalize how technically I was making good money to be able to provide a great and healthy life for a child. Besides, in our new home, we had a room that would be perfect for a nursery. Time went on and on, months went by, and it felt like my years were on repeat. Yes, I sat with these rationalizations in my head. But I also sat with my gratitude as God still gave me countless reasons to celebrate including birthdays, my husband's graduation, job promotions, and extraordinary career accomplishments that were exceptional for my age.

We had already been married almost seven years and naturally, most folks assumed that we were probably having difficulties having kids. We would get the occasional pat on the shoulder, "I'm praying for you" or "It's going to happen soon." Then there were the others who were unknowingly insensitive and would say, "Hurry up and have kids now, you're not getting any younger!" or "What are you waiting for?" or jokingly, "Is your husband shooting blanks?" Only God truly knew how we felt, and that this was a disappointing time for us that grew with each piercing comment or prodding question.

I recall making a trip to visit my parents in the Bahamas for a weekend. My mom, who is an amazing prayer warrior, invited me to go to an early morning prayer session with her prayer partners at her local church. It was an extremely early morning request, and for me not being a "morning person," I debated whether I would go. Knowing my time to visit with my parents was short, I try to indulge their requests as much as possible during my visits. It was a beautiful and simple prayer meeting with my mom and about five other ladies and their local pastor. They met every Sunday morning at about 6 a.m. to unite in prayer for various prayer requests and concerns. As I sat and listened to the prayers, my heart was encouraged and I was happy to see my mom spiritually connected and united with others in this way. As they were preparing to end someone asked me if there was anything

I wanted to have prayed for. I think this was the first time I audibly said please pray for me to have a baby. Without question or hesitation, they each began to pray on my request.

The prayers that were offered on my behalf were encouraging and uplifting and I left feeling encouraged and inspired. As we walked out of the church and were headed to our car, one of the ladies came up to us and told me she wanted to take me and my mom somewhere. We didn't have any appointments or anything else to do that morning and so we got into her car. My curiosity as to where we were headed did not last long as within about five minutes she had pulled into a clearing between a few trees that allowed us to see the ocean on the eastern end of the island.

She said the spirit led her to take us there and she also said something else which I do not remember clearly. What I do recall is that she prayed once more over both me and my mom. Immediately following her prayer, I remember looking out over the ocean and having a clear vision between where the sky met the sea of myself with three children. I almost came to tears, and in that moment I sealed God's promise with faith in my heart that someday I would be a mother.

Despite everything I experienced during this journey, my blessings are countless, the love I received is endless, I am His and I am favored!

Chapter 4

FERTILITY TREATMENT HIGHS AND LOWS

" *When you are sick, do you pray for healing? When you face a health situation like a broken leg or cancer do you seek out medical care while you pray?*

The Struggle

In 2007, we moved to a new city, and I started a new exciting job. Again life was looking great, but still no baby. We had a new fertility doctor that had amazing experience and great outcomes. We began a new series of tests and scans, but I felt something different this time. I was excited about the new possibilities of a new life and starting the family I had envisioned in my head.

After consultations with my new doctor, IVF was once again recommended as our best course of action to pursue having a child. But once again the cost was a barrier, and so we pursued the least expensive route of fertility treatment with artificial insemination. This was far from conceiving in the fun way we had planned, but not as invasive as IVF, or as costly. I thought that this must've been the way God meant for it to be for us. Unfortunately, after a few failed attempts, we accepted the fact that this was not the course of action to take. We felt we were at a dead end. We still had other financial commitments and did not feel it was the best idea to take out a loan to explore IVF fertility treatment. We were stuck as we did not want to go into debt starting out as new parents. Then there was also the risk of not having a successful pregnancy and having to live with a bill instead of living with a baby. Was God going to help us with an amazing miracle that we would testify about? We had heard other individuals share stories of how they began to explore IVF, and then "it" happened, just boom! They were pregnant and lived happily ever after. Would that be our story?

Our fervent prayers continued, "Lord please bless our home with a baby." While we prayed to God, our struggles were still private and isolated. We shared them with no one else, not even our parents at that time. There were no visible support services for our infertility struggle in our church or local community. There was also no one else we knew who could relate to our secret struggle.

After a year in my new job, a new insurance plan was introduced, and fertility treatments were covered for several attempts of fresh and frozen IVF treatments. Was this it? Was this the new path forward without going into debt? Even though I was hopeful the question of what people would think bubbled up in the back of my head. Was it the doctors that would help me to get pregnant, or was it God? Where was my faith?

These are questions I grappled with that I later learned many women grapple with too. Very often we pray and ask God for wisdom and guidance in our lives. We study His Word and believe in His power to provide. Yet, here I was guided to and provided with the opportunity to have fertility treatment, and medical assistance to help my body overcome a health challenge to conceive a child. But I was still questioning whether I was taking ownership of me fixing my fertility challenge instead of God. In His Word in James 1:17 (NIV), God then reminded me that *"Every good and perfect gift is from above, and cometh down from the Father of heavenly lights."*

Unfortunately, infertility is rarely discussed or considered a typical health issue in many settings, including some churches. Hence many couples are embarrassed to talk about it, including us. But infertility is a medical issue that requires medical care. Fertility treatment, may be needed just as physical therapy treatment is needed to aid the healing process from a broken leg, or chemotherapy to support the removal of cancer.

We finally decided to go forward with IVF treatment. There was a lot of information and steps to follow. There were the many medications, shots, the almost daily blood tests and ultrasounds, and frequent early morning doctor visits to monitor the growth of my stimulating ovaries. Everything seemed to be progressing as they told me it would, but I was still anxious and a bit nervous. It was a few days before I was scheduled for the removal of my growing eggs in my ovaries. My day started fairly normal when something went horribly wrong. I was sitting at work and the heaviness that I had in my abdomen, which was expected during this experience, suddenly turned into an incredibly deep pain. As the pain intensified, I knew something was wrong. I was working late that day when it started, and my fertility doctor's office was closed. With increasing pain, I called the after-hours number and was advised to go to the ER. The nearest hospital was only a few minutes away, but the pain made the drive feel like a million miles away. I began to become seriously worried that something bad was happening inside of me. I began to worry about whether I had ruined any opportunity to have children, was this IVF decision a bad one that I was now suffering the consequences for? When I arrived at the emergency room, they completed the intake and became aware that I was currently pursuing fertility treatment for IVF, and they took me in for an ultrasound scan immediately.

There were my eggs inside my ovaries on the screen. So many big ones on the screen. I was in awe at the potential of what I saw inside me, but the pain I had popped that bubble in my head real fast. By this time, the on-call fertility doctor at the office I went to had come to the ER. She was new at the practice but was very compassionate and knowledgeable about what was happening to me. She had reviewed the ER reports of the scans and lab work-up done. Then she told me that my ovaries were overstimulated and the eggs needed to be removed ahead of schedule. I was given some heavy pain medicine for the night, scheduled for the egg retrieval in the morning at my doctor's office, and discharged.

The eggs were removed the next morning and as was the IVF process, I was scheduled for in-vitro 3-4 days later. I was tired. I was exhausted. My body was over it but I hoped and still prayed for a good outcome to this experience. Emotionally I felt guilty and wondered if this was a form of punishment for possibly not doing it the way most folks may describe as God's way. As it would turn out, I did not get pregnant, IVF Attempt 1 was a failure!

I was sincerely disappointed and I grappled a bit with my faith. Yet I was reminded of the word of God, "...*faith by itself, if it is not accompanied by action, is dead," James 2:17 (NIV)*. So, we proceeded to schedule a second IVF cycle. This time, with a lower dose of hormones and increased monitoring, the cycle was smoother. Something was different. It was still tedious and had multiple time-consuming elements that come along with the IVF process, but this time my body and my emotions were not overwhelmed.

As I had done before, prior to my scheduled blood test to confirm if the IVF cycle had worked, I remember sitting on the couch one night and curiosity just got the better of me. Could I be pregnant yet? My period was not due for another few days and neither was the blood test at the doctor's office. But what if I was pregnant right now? Could I know? I still had a few dollar store pregnancy tests in the bathroom and so I got up and went to the bathroom and took one. With my eyes closed tight and my heartbeat pounding, I waited. They always tell you not to look before the minute had ended, but I was curious, anxious, praying. Then I remember telling myself, "If it comes back negative it's probably just too early you could still be pregnant." I'm sure the entire minute had not passed before I looked over at the test and saw a faint second pink line. I picked it up and stared. Is this right? Could it be? Am I really pregnant? Excitement started to build inside of me. Am I really, really, really pregnant? All these years of waiting and praying, were my eyes playing tricks on me Lord? I was home alone at the time of the test and could not wait for my husband to get home. But for those brief moments, I held the test, and I stared and stared at that little stick with happiness deep inside me that could not be described in words.

The next day I could hardly wait and bought a real pregnancy Test, one that did not cost a dollar, as I truly wanted to know whether it may have been a fluke.

Finally. It was my second attempt at IVF and finally, finally, I was pregnant. I WAS PREGNANT! I held in my hands for the very first time a real positive pregnancy test. The feeling was surreal, my heart was bursting with excitement, and I was simply just over the moon, filled with gratitude. Here I was praising God that after all these many years he had finally blessed my womb to have life within. I was in disbelief, I was in shock, but I was truly so happy I was ready to burst inside. I was going to be a mommy, and my amazing husband was finally going to become a dad. He would finally be able to share stories with his brother and his close cousins who already had kids, he was officially going to become a part of the daddy club and I could not be happier. Thank you, Lord!

With IVF, to confirm a viable pregnancy, hormone levels have to double after the first pregnancy blood test. While I don't recall the specific number I had, I remember when my doctor's office called me with the results after the second test stating there was no doubt, that I was pregnant, and that the probability of having twins was high given the number that was read. When I was told this, I thought for a moment how twins run in my family. My mom has a set of twin siblings, my dad has a set of twin siblings, and my dad also had two sets of twin cousins on each side of his family. Could I be the start of the next generation to bring twins into the family? I chuckled within myself holding the potential of the sweetest secret ever. I still had to wait a few weeks before an ultrasound could be scheduled to hear the heartbeat at my fertility doctor's office, but nothing could steal the joy and excitement I could hardly wait to share the news.

It was about a week after my confirmed blood pregnancy test that I was scheduled to go to Akron, Ohio on a business trip. I felt great! Then bad news arrived. One of my coolest uncles was found dead in his car slumped over his steering wheel, he had a heart attack. My family was in shock and disbelief and grief was everywhere. Then a few days later, I started spotting.

I began to panic. I called my fertility doctor's office and they said that was typical as my embryo was probably burying deep into my uterine wall and not to be concerned. I was slightly relieved until a few more days passed, and I started to have a full flow period and clots were being passed. I was already grieving for my uncle and now I began to grieve over potentially the loss of my baby that I had not yet seen on an ultrasound. I was sick to the stomach at the thought that I could be losing my baby. I could not wait any longer to go to my scheduled fertility doctor appointment for my ultrasound. I contacted my gynecologist's office for an appointment. They were able to work me in the same day. My husband was with me and holding my hand. I could tell he was just as anxiously concerned as I was by the thought of losing our first pregnancy. After all this time Lord please don't let us lose this baby. My gynecologist proceeded to do an ultrasound with a probe inserted inside of me. There was this large black sac with a little being inside and a heartbeat. Yes, a heartbeat! I began to cry and cry with everything within me. My husband and I squeezed our hands and without sharing any words we both knew how each other felt. We had a baby, and it had a heartbeat, and we could hear it. Our emotions were overflowing, mixed with confused thoughts of what was happening. I was bleeding, but I also had a baby within me with a heartbeat. My gynecologist directed me to go home and rest, and of course, the Ohio trip was canceled. I called my mom to let her know that I would not be able to travel to my uncle's funeral and shared with her for the first time that I was pregnant. I could hear the joy in her voice that helped ease some of the sorrow she was experiencing over the loss of her brother. And in her words, "Baby please just stay still no need to travel."

Happy Times Ahead
We were cautiously excited and prayed for the bleeding to stop. It gradually did. When the day of the scheduled ultrasound at the fertility doctor arrived, we were eager to reconfirm that our babies were still there, growing, alive, and well.

Yes, babies!! We had a follow-up with our gynecologist's office a week after we initially heard the heartbeat and during that visit, as they were doing the ultrasound, the doctor said, "It looks like we have another little one in here." We were in disbelief as the week prior we were just praying to have saved one and here it was we had two little beans with very strong heartbeats!!

Our fertility doctor measured both babies and checked their heart rates and they were both perfect, right around six weeks. We were ecstatic! It was truly an unbelievably happy time for my husband and me.

We lived in a two-bedroom condo and began looking online at double baby bassinets and double cribs and how they would fit in our spare bedroom. We would spend our evenings looking at reviews online for what were the best double strollers and assessing how we would adjust our work schedules around the kids.

Because I was over the age of 35, I was considered to be an advanced maternal age patient, in other words, medically I was considered older than normal to be having kids. I was therefore recommended to also have my prenatal care with a perinatologist – a high-risk prenatal doctor. Each of my appointments went great. It was the fall of 2008 and my best-friend cousin was getting married that November. As a bridesmaid in his bridal party, I was super excited for him, but I was also beaming with secret excitement as this was the first time I would be at such a grand special occasion with my babies tucked inside. The wedding was beautiful and as my cousin walked down the aisle to his soon-to-be bride he sang the song *All That's Left is to Say* by Marvin Sapp. While the lyrics of the song were for his wife, I held my flowers close to my waist and discretely rubbed my stomach, I closed my eyes and whispered the words of the song to my babies. As the evening went on, I danced, I laughed, and my husband and I took many 'first family' pictures. I remember as we were preparing to leave the reception, I pulled my grandmother aside and excitedly shared with her that her next generation was about to double as she currently had two great-granddaughters. Without words she let me know how happy she was by the news as she smiled and held my hands tight as she looked deep into my eyes. That was the cherry on the top of a fabulous day. Upon returning home after the wedding, my husband and I continued our family photoshoot with me in different poses holding my tummy. We used one of those iconic pictures that we took to make our holiday greeting cards to announce the news.

We had already made plans to spend Christmas in Memphis with my husband's family as it was his niece's first Christmas. We had just finished dinner when my husband's sister announced that she too was pregnant, and our due dates were only a week apart. The laughter, the joy, the happiness, and the excitement were beyond blissful!! My mother-in-law was beside herself, because while she was spending her first Christmas with her first granddaughter, next Christmas she would've stacked up three more to her pile of grandkids! It was an exciting time. We returned home before the New Year rolled in as we had an appointment scheduled with our perinatologist at which they were also going to reveal the sex of our babies. "It's a girl! It's a boy! Yes, yes, yes, yes!!! Look at what God has done, not only has He blessed us with one baby but two babies, not only did He bless us with a baby girl, He blessed us with a baby boy." Our family was complete.

Our season of joy and happiness continued as my husband's grandmother, his favorite aunt, and a few other relatives were in town to bring in the New Year. They invited us to spend the night with them, and as the new year rolled in we shared with them the great news! I remember my husband's grandmother laughed endlessly, with a deep belly laugh that was infectious and made everyone else laugh with her. She too was expanding her pot of great-grandchildren with her favorite grandson (while other family members may debate this, everyone knew that my husband was the apple of her eye). The year 2009 was going to be fabulous! We were happy, we finally had our babies. A girl and a boy! That was it, we were set! God had finally answered, and we were doubly blessed, for now. And then January came.

Chapter 5

A VERY COLD
JANUARY

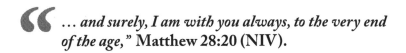 *… and surely, I am with you always, to the very end of the age,"* Matthew 28:20 (NIV).

It was January 2009, a week into the New Year, I had a business trip scheduled to Ohio. I had never visited Ohio before and was excited to check it off of my list of states to visit. My work best friend, Nicole, was along for the trip, and we were excited to share this time together, just us girls taking care of business. Having her near my side was reassuring as she had a healthcare background. I remember walking gingerly through the airport, and strangers kindly moving aside or asking if I needed help as they could see my very visible pregnant stomach. We had a direct flight from Florida. I drank lots of water and got up to stretch frequently during the flight as I recalled reading somewhere about leg blood clots during travel for pregnant women. Although I was feeling great, I was extremely cautious. We met up with our colleagues at the college in Ohio when we arrived and everything was great. We had a campus tour, good food, and then retired to our hotel for the evening. The next morning started fine. It was snowing and very cold. We got to the campus safely and began to work in an upstairs office with a few other colleagues to attend to the business we came to do. My feet were propped up on a box as I reclined a bit in the chair I was working from. Something did not feel right.

I began to feel what almost felt like small pinches on my sides. What was this? I remember excusing myself and going to the bathroom to say a prayer. Lord, please let me and my babies be okay on this trip. I shared with my work colleague what I was feeling, and she suggested calling my doctor's office, which I did. I got an automated line and left a voice message. I drank more water and sat back down. The sensation ended. I remember reassuring myself in my head, *you're taking it easy, just continue to remain still and relaxed and comfortable in this chair, you're good.* I did just that, I remained still, sat reclined, and kept my legs crossed and propped up on a box. I thought to myself, *There, I'm good. I'm comfortable, the pinching sensation was gone, I'm good!*

Our meeting with our Ohio colleagues continued with ease. There were about eight of us, all men except for me, Nicole, and another female instructor at the college. Despite our gender differences, they were not just professional but kind. Our meeting conversations were productive and cordial and then out of nowhere, a gush! A gush of warm water fell down my legs. I reached for and squeezed Nicole's hand and cried, "Call 911, my babies!" I don't know who called 911, but everyone cleared the room except for Nicole who stayed by my side. While fearing the worst, I remained calm and took slow breaths while trying to keep my legs closed as tight as possible.

It felt as if the paramedics got there fairly quickly, and the conversation began on how best to get me to the ambulance as we were on the second floor of the building and there was not an elevator. I remember one of my Ohio colleagues who had returned to the room explaining the layout of the building to the paramedics and describing that the room we were in was near the back. The paramedics sent a radio message for the ambulance to come to the back of the building. I was then gently, very gently, lifted onto a stretcher and strapped in with lots of blankets. Somehow there was a form of a conveyor that was placed on the stairs that my stretcher was placed onto, and I was gently lowered down the stairs at an angle with several paramedics by my side. I remember telling the paramedics a few times, I felt as if I was sliding off or sliding down and they reassured me that I was safely secured to the stretcher. I remember that as we reached the bottom I could see thick white snow falling, there were several students wearing heavy winter jackets that stood off to the side, likely curious as to what was happening. Nicole was now no longer by my side, but she promised me as they were taking me down the stairs that she would meet me at the hospital.

There I was, alone, just me and my babies in the back of the ambulance in snowy Ohio. But the word of God on repeat in my head kept whispering "I am with you always." Where are they taking me? What is happening? Are my babies okay? I was cool as a cucumber on the outside, but my brain was going a mile a minute gravely concerned for my babies. I wasn't in any pain, but I was truly confused by what just happened. I could still feel my babies moving inside of me and the paramedics said all my vitals checked were okay. So, what just happened? As I was lifted out of the ambulance and carried into the emergency room, I remember a doctor stated they were using a strip to test the fluid on me to determine whether I had peed myself or whether it was amniotic fluid from my babies. Unfortunately, it was amniotic fluid and they had me moved right away to an ultrasound room. There were my babies! They were there on the screen once more, happy and rolling around living their best life inside me and they looked great. My precious Azaria and DJ both looked fine.

The ultrasound technician then let me know that my son DJ had lost most of his amniotic fluid. "Would my body generate more fluid?" I asked. "Are they doing okay?" The technician let me know the doctor would discuss my options more with me. As I was being wheeled back to the emergency evaluation room, Nicole came running to meet me. I was relieved to see her. She had kept my phone and belongings and I was eager to call my husband. She let me know that she had called him to let him know what happened and that my company was working on getting him a flight to Ohio as soon as possible.

I began to pray within me and cried softly for God to please let my babies be okay. My friend Nicole was not a Christian and we had had many intriguing debates on life, God, and miracles. I thought to myself, God this would be a perfect time for Nicole to see your miraculous power at work, and also the power of prayer. The ER doctor came in and let me know that unfortunately my son DJ had lost quite a bit of his amniotic fluid. And that there was a high probability of me losing him because if I continued to lose fluid, he would not have a sufficient amount to survive. I was admitted to the hospital that night. After Nicole left, there I was, alone in a strange sterile hospital room hooked up to many machines that were being used to monitor my vitals and my babies. I prayed. While I was concerned for the safety of my babies, I don't think I ever fully processed the thought of them not surviving the pregnancy. My thoughts instead went to whether this hospital had the capacity to care for them if I stayed here long enough or if there was an option to be airlifted back to Florida. Then I prayed, "God, I know you did not bring me and my babies this far to leave us now." I'm sure I was given some form of sedative as I recall drifting off to sleep and resting pretty well that first night in the hospital. I woke early the next morning to a specialist who came in to evaluate me and she made me aware of my risks. That didn't matter to me, I just wanted my babies to be safe.

My main goal was to save my babies, whatever we had to do; I just wanted to save my babies. My company flew my husband to Ohio to be with me and a colleague picked him up at the airport and brought him to the hospital. I was relieved to see him, but I also had a mix of emotions. He was mostly concerned that I was okay and wanted for me to be well, but I was disheartened because I was beginning to feel I was at fault for what had happened. Maybe if I had not gone on this business trip, I would not be laying here placing our babies' lives at risk, I thought. My husband however was reassuring me that was not his concern. He just wanted me to relax, be comfortable, and be safe. My main concern then shifted to asking my nurses if I was at the right hospital or if there another hospital that had specialized doctors to help me save this pregnancy.

As my second day in the hospital continued, the doctors who tended to me let me know that I had lost quite a bit of fluid around one of the babies and there was a high risk of me delivering him early. I began to worry, as I knew I was too early to deliver. At this stage of my pregnancy, my son would not be viable and not have any chance of survival. There were a lot of prayers, as we called almost everyone we could think of to pray. "Lord, please save our babies! We went through so much to get here, please don't leave us now."

As my second evening came, the white from the snow falling outside my window turned to the dark of night literally and figuratively. I went into labor. A series of beeping machines and a flurry of activity were all around me. I remember crying. Not because I was in pain, but I was pleading with them to keep me from delivering my babies. I don't remember being in pain, but I do remember becoming fearful of what my body was doing as I lay there helpless. Just the night before when I was admitted and taken to my room, I remember asking the nurse if I could be reclined slightly in a way that would elevate my butt and lower my head so as to not create pressure on my cervix. She did. Tonight however the machine beeped as I felt the bed lower in the opposite direction. I cried, "Please God no, no, no."

I can still remember the feeling as my son, my DJ, in one big movement came sliding out of me. I knew he was gone. I refocused my energy on my baby girl as they took him away. I cried for him in my heart, but I cried audibly for my daughter, "Please save my baby girl. Jesus, please save my baby girl." I was overwhelmed with grief and emotions, but I felt as if there was a presence near the side of my head. It felt as if God was in the room next to me. So I kept crying out, "Please, please, God save my baby girl please save my baby girl." As I turned my head, I saw the nurse place something in my IV line that I assume was some form of sedative.

I don't remember anything after that cry, until the next morning when I woke up and I knew she was gone. She was gone. I don't have any recollection of her birth or anything, but I was empty. My babies both were no longer within me. I no longer felt any movement. As I opened my eyes, the room was empty except for my husband sitting in a chair next to my bed. He gave a brave smile and asked how I was feeling. With tears falling down my face, I had no words for him. After a short while, I asked him where was Azaria, although I knew the answer. He said she was gone as he held my hand. I asked him what happened as I had a blank spot in my memory either from the trauma of the night or sedatives I had received. He then described that I delivered her a few minutes after DJ. He shared that she was still in her sac when she was born and that he was able to see her for a short while before she was taken away. He described that she was beautiful, and then he told me that he cried. I had never seen my husband cry before. Knowing that the heartbreak of seeing our daughter taken away made him cry tore my heart up inside.

Again it was a new morning, I was in mourning and all I could see was white out my hospital window. The snow was so heavy. There was so much snow and as my husband was holding my hand, I was empty. I didn't feel anything. I didn't feel my babies anymore. We just held each other's hands, and we were silent. "Did this just really happen, God?"

It was not very long before one of my nurses came in to check my vitals. She asked me if I wanted to see my babies. I whispered yes. A few minutes later, they wheeled my babies into the room in the bassinet. My nurse was very gentle and very compassionate. She asked if I wanted to hold them, and I said yes. They were wrapped in hospital baby blankets and had little knitted caps on. She placed them in my arms. As my husband looked on by my side, I soaked in the reality that I was holding my DJ and Azaria. I was holding my babies. I got to pray over them and I let them know how much I loved them and how much joy they had brought to our life. I kissed them goodbye.

During this time, I know that many people were praying for me, some who called to pray with me. There was a pastor from a local church who came to visit with me; he knew someone who knew me. The pastor said he felt it was important to come and visit and pray with me. Somehow I felt the power of God's presence comforting and keeping me in a way that I cannot explain in words. It was like a soothing powerful presence was in my hospital room and it reminded me of the same presence that was next to my head when I delivered my son. I began to sing the songs *Trust in God*, and *There is a Sweet, Sweet Spirit in This Place*.

My heart was shattered into little pieces, but somehow I received divine strength to smile through my tears. Several of my nurses expressed that they were witnessing something they had never seen before in a person who had experienced such a loss. To this day I sometimes wonder if my experience was there to reach the souls of those I encountered in the hospital for God. I know He was there in the midst of my pain. I was very eager to leave Ohio and return home. We decided to cremate our babies. I remember being wheeled out of the hospital, cold and clutching the urn that was engraved with my children's names. A taxi pulled up and took us directly to the airport. I brought our babies' ashes home to Florida.

The days and weeks that followed are sometimes a blur. I remember the love that we received from my church family who brought food and held a beautiful memorial service for our babies. I remember the comfort in my soul that God was still with me. My pastor at that time based the eulogy for the memorial on Isaiah 41:17-20 (NIV):

> *The poor and needy search for water, but there is none; their tongues are parched with thirst. But I the Lord will answer them; I, the God of Israel, will not forsake them. I will make rivers flow on barren heights, and springs within the valleys. I will turn the desert into pools of water, and the parched ground into springs. I will put in the desert the cedar and the acacia, the myrtle and the olive. I will set junipers in the wasteland, the fir and the cypress together, so that people may see and know, may consider and understand, that the hand of the Lord has done this, that the Holy One of Israel has created it.*

"My time will come, I will someday be a mom," I prayed, "And someday everyone will know, it was the hand of the Lord that had done it!"

Chapter 6

SHE'S PREGNANT, NOT ME

> *... Be agreeable, be sympathetic, be loving, be compassionate, be humble. That goes for all of you, no exceptions, No retaliation. No sharp-tongued sarcasm. Instead, bless – that's your job, to bless. You'll be a blessing and also get a blessing,"* 1 Peter 3:8 (MSG).

I wasn't ready...

About six weeks had passed and my doctor had cleared me to return to work. I was nervous but ready to move forward. I didn't know what to expect or feel but I knew I needed to go back to work. I entered my workplace. I can still see the smile of our receptionist who said it's nice to see you again. As I walked past others there was a gentle nod and smile and gratefully nobody asked me how I was feeling. Looking back I'm grateful for the compassion, respect for my privacy, and the space which my office colleagues had extended to me. During this time I shared an office with my work colleague Nicole, who had traveled with me to Ohio. She greeted me with a warm hug and I could feel the deep love and compassion in her embrace. It was comforting. As I sat down and looked around my desk everything was the same. My calendar had notes for doctor's appointments and other reminders that I began to slowly clear from my desk. It was only a few minutes that I was seated before Nicole shared with me that she had something important to tell me. I didn't think much of it as I just assumed it was work-related. I looked up and turned in her direction, and without a moment's notice she blurted, "I'm pregnant."

Before this, she was not even trying to get pregnant. She was not even pregnant when I had lost my babies. Yet, here I was on my first day back to work with the realization that I would be working side-by-side with her. She's pregnant, not me. She was pregnant and excited, so I was happy for her. However, this did not diminish the pain and grief I was experiencing over the loss of my babies and the challenges I had to conceive. Nicole would occasionally make comments to encourage me by saying, "have fun trying again." But, she only knew half of my struggle. How is this supposed to work for the next nine months? She was with me when it happened in Ohio. Looking back, I know now that God was not telling me no. He was just saying not yet.

After my pregnancy loss with the twins, I had a long talk with God requesting if I were to experience such heartache again, I would prefer him not to allow my womb to carry another child. Yes, I said that! The hurt and anguish I felt after everything I went through to conceive the twins was so deep, that I did not want to go through it again. And so I made a pact with God (at least I thought I did). Lord, if I were to become pregnant again, that pregnancy would come to fruition. We tried again and failed.

The grieving process was difficult, I cried for my babies for many days as I reflected on what life would have been like with them. My sister-in-law who I had shared the joyous holidays with and who I looked forward to mutually sharing baby delivery stories with, gave birth to a beautiful daughter in June 2009. I remember the night her baby was delivered. We sat on the phone with relatives who were at the hospital waiting with great anticipation for the news of my niece's arrival. I was excited about the birth of my niece. Yet, I still longed for my babies and dreamt of what it would've been like for my twins to share the same birth month with her.

A few weeks after losing the twins, my doctors discussed how I had a few fibroids that had grown larger during my pregnancy. Although there was no evidence to directly correlate whether it impacted my pregnancy loss, they were concerned that it could negatively impact future pregnancies. The thought of another hurdle was frustrating. My doctor strongly recommended that before proceeding with another IVF cycle, I consider having a myomectomy (having my fibroids removed), as a precaution. I was extremely nervous about this given my concern for additional scar tissue buildup should I have another surgery. My doctor reassured me that the location of my fibroids was external to my uterine cavity and that once I had healed from the procedure, within approximately two or three months, I should be okay to try again. He advised me not to be concerned about scar tissue buildup which usually occurs after more time had passed.

I sat each day next to my colleague as her belly grew. I watched her excitement as she went through the motions of a soon-to-be mom. Simultaneously, I was getting over the hurdle of my loss and moving forward with trying again. Additionally, I was now having to factor in fibroid removal before I could join in her journey. I never shared with her the challenges I was facing, as I did not want to take away from the joy she was experiencing. I was happy for her. However, my path to becoming a mom just felt like one more big hurdle to jump over. My faith was encouraged by knowing that I could become pregnant and knowing there were others now standing in the gap of prayer for me. I was at peace, and we made the decision to proceed with the surgery.

With the confidence of knowing we could get pregnant now on our side, we wanted to remove any challenges that will prevent our next pregnancy from being successful.

I was relieved that I made it through another procedure. "Thank you, Jesus, I woke up again," I thought to myself, still groggy from the procedure. I felt my abdomen as my hands grazed over the staples. Did it work, were all the fibroids gone, was my womb still ok?

My following post-op appointments had a good prognosis. I healed great. Now all the obstacles that would get in the way of a successful pregnancy were gone (at least so I thought). I was ready! We were ready! We knew the drill. We told ourselves, "It's going to happen this time. Let's go get pregnant!"

The surgery was successful. But it was not that simple. The subsequent months that followed were filled with scans, needles, logs, and now questions. I was not getting pregnant! Would it ever happen again? I remember my husband appeared cool on the outside about everything, but I knew he was also feeling disappointed. He rarely showed his emotions but with his signature sheepish smile, he would just gently hold my hand and whisper it's going to happen. Don't worry it's going to happen, babe. It was as if at times God was speaking through my husband to reassure me of the promised vision He had given to me in February 2007.

I do not recall the number of times we tried. I remember clearly being anxious to know if IVF worked. I secretly used my dollar store pregnancy test stash repeatedly before each scheduled beta pregnancy test at the doctor's office. I wanted to see if I got that magical extra line. Where was my *Faith INfertility*?

Eventually, the doctors and I began to question why my embryos were not implanting. I was scheduled for an endometrial biopsy. This began a new journey. My endometrial journey in my current infertility journey.

With my first biopsy, I was diagnosed with endometritis. I had heard of endometriosis before, but I was a bit confused as to what this meant. Eventually, my doctor explained to me that it was an inflammation of my endometrial lining which is where an embryo is implanted for pregnancy to occur. My doctor advised that it would not be beneficial for me to proceed with IVF again until this was cleared. Again! Another hurdle! I was prescribed a 10-day round of antibiotic treatment and my menstrual cycle was required to pass before I was able to have a follow-up biopsy. In essence, the process was a full month.

The endometrial biopsy was one of my most physically painful procedures during my infertility challenges. It involved my doctor inserting a medical instrument in me that would take a pinch of my uterine lining tissue to be tested. Although usually they were pinches, not a pinch. He always wanted to ensure he got sufficient tissue samples of my uterine lining for the biopsy. This resulted in me having to remain still for at least 15 minutes as I gathered my emotions for the painful invasion of my uterus to get an endometrial sample. I eventually came to realize the value of pain relievers as I popped two to three ibuprofen pills before each biopsy. They helped to 'reduce' the pain I had afterward. The timing of the endometrial biopsy could only happen once a month approximately 10 days after my menstrual period.

My life became a drumbeat based on a monthly menstrual rhythm– menstrual flow, biopsy, wait for results, positive for endometritis, antibiotic treatment, menstrual flow, biopsy, wait for results, positive for endometritis, and on repeat it went, until finally, finally, I was negative. I was almost as excited to receive a negative test, as I was to receive a positive pregnancy test. Ironic right? While there is no scientific evidence to support what I will share next, I did eliminate meat from my diet which consisted of mostly chicken. To this day, I sometimes believe that may have played a factor in my body's inability to allow the antibiotic treatment to resolve the inflammation in my uterus.

Finally, it happened, the big fat negative we had been waiting on that would allow us to try once more. Again, the irony is that we all celebrate and look forward to the big fat positive – BFP (for our pregnancy test while trying to become pregnant), and here I was looking forward to the big fat negative - BFN.

Without hesitation, we were ready to have a fresh IVF cycle. We prayed!! We were excited about the opportunity to try again. I reflected on the pact that I had made with God; if He were to allow me to get pregnant one more time, this next pregnancy would be full-term and end with a beautiful living and breathing baby in my arms.

In October 2009, I arrived at the hospital in the evening. Nicole had given birth to a beautiful baby girl, Alia. After she was delivered, I held her close and prayed over her life, grateful for her safe arrival.

Chapter 7

GOD, DID YOU FORGET ME?

" *So do not fear, for I am with you; do not be dismayed, for I am your God. Will strengthen you and help you; I will uphold you with my righteous right hand,"* Isaiah 41:10 (NIV).

Another pregnancy loss and we took a break from trying.

We were eager with anticipation and ready to move past hearing the line, "Sorry, but the last round of antibiotic treatment didn't work as your uterine lining biopsy still is testing positive for endometritis." That line had begun to sound like a tape recorder gone bad month after month each time we heard my fertility doctor sharing these words. Somewhere deep inside I sometimes wondered if God was about to perform a natural miracle experience within me and wondered if that was His original plan and I was just not hearing it. Although I could not see anything that remotely resembled a miracle for me at that time. Little did I realize that I was on a miraculous journey of *Faith INfertility* orchestrated by God.

A year had now passed since I said goodbye to my twins, the fibroids were gone, the endometritis was gone, but still no baby. My husband, however, was a solid rock who was beyond supportive and just said "It's going to happen baby," no pun intended.

I don't recall how many times we attempted, but we were still in the window of IVF attempts allowed by my new insurance plan. I began to wonder whether God had answered the pact I made with Him regarding not letting me become pregnant if there was a chance that I would not have the baby at full term. Maybe He was protecting me from the heartache I had experienced with my twins. Let's go one more time! The needles, the scans, the early morning bloodwork appointments, and all the grueling mental energy that pursuing fertility treatment involves continued. And then...the thought of God not allowing us to have another pregnancy faded. I finally held again my dollar store pregnancy test with a faint pretty pink second line! Oh yes Lord, thank you!! I'm finally pregnant, again! The vision!

How could I have doubted! How could I have ever made a pact with God that did not align with the vision He had given me before. I was excited but cautiously optimistic as I still needed to take my beta pregnancy test at my doctor's office. The beta pregnancy test involved having two blood tests, several days apart, to ensure my hormones were increasing at the levels needed to have a successful pregnancy. It happened and I was given the greenlight. I was officially pregnant again. Yes, Lord! Thank you, God! You gave us a second chance, and you promised that if I should get pregnant again, we would have our baby, right?

There was no spotting! Check! I felt great! Check! There was a little bean of life growing inside me again! Check! Not having any blood spotting episodes while we waited for our pregnancy ultrasound was reassuring. We were eager and ready the morning our ultrasound was scheduled. As the ultrasound probe was inserted, we could clearly see the sac our little baby was in. That black glob spot was round and perfect, then with a slight adjustment, there laying at the bottom of the sac was a beautiful little bean. Now for the heartbeat...we heard it! It was there! My husband and I squeezed hands as the doctor continued his measurements and various checks.

We got our beautiful pictures of the ultrasound printed and handed to us. The doctor then turned to us and said that while everything looked good, the baby's heartbeat was a bit weaker than it should be at this stage. My heart sank a bit. But as he continued talking he did say it was still early or it could just be developing a bit late. Of course, that was what it was, my baby was here and growing. Only one this time, but my baby is tucked away inside and growing. The heartbeat will be stronger the next time. We were scheduled to return within a week for one more scan before we were to be released to our OB/GYN doctor.

Time went by so slowly that week, but we were delighted at our second appointment to hear our doctor say that our baby's heartbeat was much stronger. Yes, our new son or daughter had found their place in my womb and here I was again. Finally, pregnant.

A few days later, one of my best girlfriends shared with me the news of her pregnancy. I was finally going to have someone else to share this journey with again, I was excited for us. We shared happy silly pregnancy stories of how we were gagging when we brushed our teeth and how we were feeling. We were just beside ourselves excited that we were on this pregnancy journey together. We were having so much fun!

Because of my age and my past pregnancy loss, I was considered to be a high-risk pregnancy patient and so we wanted the best prenatal care. We already decided that travel was not going to be considered anywhere until after I had delivered. We were scheduled to see a perinatologist at a high-risk pregnancy facility that was the best in town. Walking inside, we met a concierge and other amazing features of the facility that made us feel like we were in a fancy hotel instead of a medical facility. We were excited!

We completed the regular paperwork. I went into a private room where an ultrasound tech came to begin our initial scan. I adjusted myself on the table leaning back relaxed but still somewhat anxious. She began to move the probe around, and around and around and around. I adjusted myself as I waited to hear my baby's heartbeat. The tech who was talkative at first became silent as she continued to take the measurements. Measurements of the sac, measurements of my baby, and then on she went with the probe again around and around and around. I asked quietly, "can I hear the baby's heartbeat yet?" The screen was turned slightly away from me, but I was able to see slightly just a straight line on the area where I knew the heartbeat should have been. I asked her again, can I hear the baby's heartbeat, please? She then said the doctor would be in to talk with me about the baby soon, and then walked out. As soon as she left I took the liberty to adjust the screen a bit more in my direction to see more clearly what was happening when the doctor returned.

I was becoming nervous. My husband and I sat silently while we waited until the doctor entered the room. It was our first time meeting him, but we felt we knew him as we were told he was one of the best and we had done our research on him as well. He greeted us professionally but didn't waste time getting right to the scan as the ultrasound technician stood directly behind him.

He turned to us and firmly said, "I'm sorry, there is no heartbeat." Time literally stood still and my heart began to race, it felt like 1,000 beats per minute. I firmly replied although I know my voice was quivering, please check again. He turned the screen toward us and moved the probe around and around. This time, not only did we not hear a heartbeat, we did not see any movement. My baby was not moving.

I was in shock but wanted to leave as quickly as possible. I refused to accept what he was saying or what I thought I was seeing. My husband was seated in silence the entire time. I don't recall any other words the doctor or the technician shared after that, but know that they walked out of the room to give us privacy and for me to get dressed. Dear God, no! The devil was a liar once more. It absolutely had to be a mistake.

I was dressed and ready to leave, my husband got up to take my hand and help me, but instead, he stumbled back into the chair and fainted. I panicked, ran to the door and shouted for help. In seconds, the doctor and technician returned and were able to revive him. Dear God, what was happening? First, the enemy was trying to steal my baby, and now my husband!

To this day, we're still not sure whether it was the shock of the news, or whether he was still exhausted from having worked that night prior to our visit, or both. After a few minutes of resting and drinking some juice, his vitals were fine and he said he felt much better. I drove us both home. I was not accepting this; I had a pact with God!

My refusal led me to schedule an ultrasound at another facility two days later, but this time I went alone. I had no signs of miscarrying, I never spotted once, but here I was once more laying on the table looking at an ultrasound screen with my little angel asleep, gone, with no movement, no heartbeat. Where was my God?

Within a week we scheduled a dilation and curettage surgical procedure, also called a D&C for the removal of my deceased Angel. How could you have let this happen to me again, Lord? Why was this happening to me? Was my faith in God, my faith in becoming pregnant, becoming a mother, not in God's will? What about the vision?

There were only a select few who were aware that I had become pregnant a second time. My mom, Miss Joni, Mom Bev, and two close friends. However, when I lost my angel, who we later learned was a baby girl, my parents shared the news with our family because I was unable to travel for a family event that I would have normally attended. The procedure was the week before Father's Day weekend and our wedding anniversary. We had made plans to spend our wedding anniversary in Saint Augustine on the beach, just us rubbing my tummy and reflecting on God's blessing on my womb a second time. Clearly, God didn't have that in His plans for us, and now I felt in my head that I needed space from Him. I had so many questions, I was hurting so deeply. Was my faith in God all wrong?

The last time I went through this experience, I came out heartbroken, but with a faith strong as a fortress knowing the God that I believed in, and knowing that He was with me. This time was different. It is so important to belong to a village of Christian believers when going through life's darkest moments. This time, I had entered a season where I could not pray for myself. I strongly believe that it was because of the prayers of those standing in the gap for me during this time that I eventually made it out of that dark season to renew my faith in God.

Father's Day came. I called my uncles to extend my greetings, and my Uncle Dan extended his sympathy for what he knew I was experiencing. He then echoed the following words that still sit in my heart today, "Baby girl, this experience you were going through is not for you but for someone else." At that moment, that statement made absolutely no sense to me, but being respectful, I said happy Father's Day Uncle and ended the conversation.

There was a World Church Conference being held in Atlanta the first week of July. My mom and a close friend had traveled to the event, and strongly encouraged me to attend but I wanted nothing to do with church or God. I just needed and wanted to be alone. I remember it was a Friday night. I decided that I would watch part of the conference event online. There was a special feature regarding the books of a renowned Christian author, Ellen G. White (EGW). During the special feature there was a booth where they were selling her books at the conference and were noting how her books for the first time were available for free online via the EGW app.

I thought to myself, *my husband would probably be interested in getting a set of her books* and decided to download the app and the books on his mobile device while he was at work that evening.

The next day, my heart was still aching for all my babies that I had lost. I was heartbroken. I decided to go for a walk with my dog, beginning to accept that maybe he would be the only baby I was to have. Many people have four-legged kids and live a full life of happiness. Maybe that was going to be my life too. While I was telling myself this in my head, deep within my soul I knew this was not true. But where was God? I grabbed my dog's leash and we headed for our walk. And for the first time in a few weeks, I began to talk to God and let Him know how angry I felt, how disappointed I was, and how He had forsaken and forgotten me. Yes that was it! I was His forgotten child who had given her entire life to Him. Why have you forsaken me? Why have you forgotten me Lord? I kept repeating that as I walked my dog around our neighborhood.

My husband, who had been napping when I went for a walk, was awake when I came in. We had a small meal and then he said let's have a small devotion as he could probably sense my resentment and separation from God. I let him know about the books I downloaded the night before. He thought it would be a great idea to read one of the books, and so we did. We prayed and he began to read the first chapter of the first book by White, *The Acts of the Apostles*:[1]

> *"In an acceptable time have I heard thee ... for He that hath mercy on them shall lead them, even by the springs of water shall He guide them. And I will make all My mountains a way, and My highways shall be exalted ... Sing, O heavens; and be joyful, O earth; and break forth into singing, O mountains: for the Lord hath comforted His people, and will have mercy upon His afflicted. But Zion said, The Lord hath forsaken me, and my Lord hath forgotten me. Can a woman forget her sucking child, that she should not have compassion on the son of her womb? yea, they may forget, yet will I not forget thee. Behold, I have graven thee upon the palms of My hands; thy walls are continually before Me," Isaiah 49:8-16 (KJV).*

As my husband read, it was as if God himself with speaking in my head telling me, a mother may forget her child, but I will not forget you, because you are written on the palms of my hands. The palms of your hands God? My life is continually before you? I broke down in tears as I shared with my husband that I just had told God how I had felt so forgotten and forsaken. Yet, here it was; He had used the books I had downloaded the night before to directly speak to me to remind me that He had not forgotten me and that my life was written in the palms of His hands. How often do you look at your hands? The thought that my life is written on His hands overwhelmed me! Coming to a self-understanding of the spiritual place I had entered during this season was new. I had many questions. Many questions that were unanswered and still remain unanswered.

---

[1] White, E. G. (1911). *The Acts of the Apostles*. Mountain View, CA: Pacific Press Publishing Association.

Becoming comfortable with unanswered questions from this experience was challenging, but I learned it was necessary for me to completely put my trust in God. Joyce Meyers writes, "We need to become comfortable with unanswered questions when we do not understand what is happening in our lives,"[2] (*Trusting God Day By Day*, 2012, p. 34).

[2] Meyers, J. (2012). *Trusting God Day By Day (First Edition)*. FaithWords.

Chapter 8

FAITH INFERTILITY

❝ *I am the LORD thy God, who brought you up out of Egypt: Open wide your mouth, and I will fill it,"*
Psalm 81:10 (NIV).

Artificial insemination … check, fertility tests … check, IVF… check, genetic testing… check, cystectomy … check, myomectomy (fibroid removals)… check, HSG, repeated endometrial biopsy … check, check, check, check; repeated miscarriages … check, my faith at this point … question mark.

Have you ever struggled with the thought of whether your faith, your conviction, or your belief that God would bring something through on your behalf; yet it never came to pass, and then you wondered if your faith truly aligned with the will of God?

Several months had passed. Time was moving slower than a turtle trying to cross the road. Life was at a standstill like traffic waiting for the turtle to reach the other side. I was lying in a bathtub of warm water at the end of another work week questioning where my faith intersected with the will of God. Lord, you said if I have faith the size of a mustard seed I could move mountains. I believed with every fiber of my being that my last pregnancy would result in a healthy baby. There was never a doubt in my mind. Was that not faith? It was my perspective that everything that transpires aligns with the will of God. So was my faith not in alignment with God's will? I struggled deeply to make these two terms congruent.

There were many days I was in a mindful state of isolation in my thoughts on faith. The secrets of my fragile faith was invisible to those around me. As a form of encouragement, there were family and friends who believed that I was still grieving the loss of my twins and they would share stories of how other couples had miscarriages and eventually went on to have children. They encouraged me to have kids, to try again. They said many people have miscarriages in their first pregnancies. They said it will happen with your next pregnancy. However, what they did not realize was that they only knew half the story. I was trying, and trying, and trying and it was not happening. I was carrying the pain of a double burden; the inability to get pregnant and the fear of another miscarriage. This sucked! But through the pain, a still voice constantly whispered in my ear and echoed a text that has always strengthened my faith on this journey, "…I am with you always" Matthew 28:20 (NIV).

I was physically, mentally, and spiritually exhausted, and because I had not normalized the thought of infertility in my life, my faith was without a foundation in this area. As a couple we struggled privately with this. There were no 'visible' outlets, communities, or couples that shared in our challenges. This was our secret, and our faith, that was being tested, could barely hold the weight of it.

While sometimes it is perfectly okay to hurt privately; it is important to recognize that couples are not alone. Couples should be free to share and grow *INfaith INfertility* publicly as a testimony of what God can do. In life we sometimes get news that is unbearable to conceive, figuratively and literally! Life and its curveballs make it difficult to understand what is happening when the doctor's report is confusing. But as the popular song title by Ron Kenoly asks, *Whose Report Shall You Believe?* I questioned myself often, "do I believe God's report that I was healed, filled, free, and have victory? While grappling with my *Faith INfertility* journey, again I asked myself, "Whose report will you believe?"

"I'm sorry but the only recommendation I have left is for you to consider surrogacy. We've been through this several times already and sometimes we are unable to determine why a couple is not able to conceive or carry a pregnancy to term." These were the final words of our reproductive endocrinologist who had been our fertility specialist for the past four years. I recall he pulled out a book that reflected a case study proving to us that this mystery sometimes occurs with couples. Here we were again as he went over the unfortunate outcome of my most recent miscarriage and my history of failed fertility options. Yes, 4 years with this doctor and one year with another, and still no baby.

We finally decided it was time to take a break. Just focus on us, and not think about a baby or when it would happen. We entered the year 2011 shifting our mindset completely on enjoying life and preparing to celebrate our 10th wedding anniversary. I still had moments where my mind would think about everyone else that was experiencing motherhood. I recalled a story my grand aunt shared with me about a couple that had been married 12 years before they had their first baby. It was time for us to move on. We had stopped all forms of fertility treatments and appointments and instead booked flights, tours, and cruises. No more tests, no more baby talks, just us and life, full and free. Initially, the thought of delaying our efforts to try was disheartening, but we knew our lives and our faith needed refreshment. Around this time, I was also struggling with constant pain in my hands, and multiple doctors were unable to determine a cause for it. With hands like these, how would I be able to care for a baby anyhow? This was another area of my life that was filled with a myriad of tests and appointments as I was unable to turn a door handle or even button my blouse without severe pain. My medical chart with the orthopedic doctor was closed almost simultaneously with our decision to put our fertility treatment attempts on hold.

My Mom Bev's doctor friend was visiting about this time and recommended for me to consider a gluten-free diet for the pain in my hands. In 2011, being gluten-free was not as trendy as it is now, but I decided to give it a try. Within two months of starting this diet, I began to notice breaks in my pain. Eventually, those breaks resulted in consistent relief over time.

Our break from everything continued with our 10th wedding anniversary celebration that took us to explore Europe on a Mediterranean cruise. Imagine that cruise on a gluten-free diet. The diet was an adjustment, but the food overall was still great. We focused on the reality that we shared a beautiful love and life that many wished they could have.

Despite our grief, we were grateful for God having sustained our marriage through the challenges of *Faith INfertility*.

My faith was refreshed and renewed. The prayers of many carried and lifted my faith through this season. I came to acknowledge and profess, that if God did not bless our life any more than He had blessed us, we had been blessed more than enough. My *Faith INfertility* was renewed. Through this journey, I've come to learn that God loves to respond to faith. I've come to know that God responds to our tested faith and sometimes he does that through the delivery of a delayed promise - not delayed by his standards, but delayed by ours. Because God never delays what he has purposefully timed for a specific point in our lives.

Chapter 9

THE TRANSITION

" *... and you give them their food at the proper time,"*
Psalm 145:15 (NIV).

We had entered a new season.

It was our 10th wedding anniversary year. Our Mediterranean anniversary cruise was absolutely fabulous. We wore matching outfits, toured Barcelona, Nice, Florence, Monaco, and Rome. We were beginning to thrive in our careers and the love and sincere relationships we had with family and friends. We were exceptionally grateful for our life. We were also on a quest to have a deeper connection with God. For me, that was making sure before I did anything else, I was following His will for my life. It had been almost a year since we had the 'baby talk.' It was a good break mentally and physically for my mind, body, and soul.

During this time my internal struggles regarding what next steps God wanted me to take regarding fertility treatment were beginning to reach their peak. I wanted to know and do exactly what God wanted for me and not what I thought was best. There were days when my soul would hunger and thirst for God to tell me what to do. It was painful in my soul. I wanted to hear from Him, and I wanted to follow Him. I wanted to do His will and not mine. There were moments when I began to wonder if my baby losses were in any way consequential to my not truly being in tune with His guidance in my life. My soul thirsted for His direction. I recall reading in His word that He freely and liberally gives wisdom to all men, and I begged Him to give this wisdom to me.

As my husband and I frequently studied the Bible and had devotion together, he would periodically ask "where" I was. I knew he was trying to understand, where I was mentally when he asked that question. He reminded me of the importance and value of writing down all the great things that God has done in our lives.

I knew he was right. He encouraged me to take notes. He told me that when we face challenges we could look back on what we have written and be encouraged. By writing about overcoming my past struggles, I would be able to rejoice because I had the confirmation of what was written down as evidence of how great God truly is. It was shortly after my husband prompted me to begin writing that my inner desire to get a journal was ignited. It was a September morning in 2011 on my way to work that the song by Fred Hammond played on my car radio. "… and if he says the land is ours we should move ahead, with no delay because we are more than able." As the song played, I was reminded that at sunrise the same morning I had awoken to a still voice in my head. I was confident that the still voice I had heard was from the Holy Spirit of God, directing me on what I was to do next. It was time to move forward. It was now time to consider the next round of IVF.

God was now providing me confirmation through this song. On the same day when I entered my office, there was a beautiful brown journal that was engraved *Trust in the Lord*, sitting on my desk. I had never spoken about the need for a journal or a desire for a journal with anyone except my husband. Yet, on the same morning I had received confirmation from God through a still voice, a song on my radio, and now an unexpected journal. Combining these events was confirming the need for me to trust in the Lord and to write the next steps of this journey that God was taking me on. The journal was left on my desk by a team member who said that she had it for several months, but was prompted to give it to me on that day. In my heart, I thanked God for providing me with these confirmation signs to give me peace as I prepared for the transition of this new season.

During the next few months, my hunger and thirst for a deeper relationship with God grew stronger, and I began to feel His presence fill me up. There were also moments when

I felt like His presence in my life was overflowing. I began to write! I began to write a lot in my new journal. I began to constantly receive spiritual affirmations of His direction for my life. His joy, peace, and love began to show up tangibly for me through various individuals and my daily study in His word. The way I began to feel left me never wanting to leave God's presence. I was secretly wrapped in His peace. I also began to feel His peace in the decision to move forward with IVF. It was a peace that transcended my understanding and led me to repeatedly say in prayer, "Lord if you never bless me any more than you have at this point, I am blessed more than enough."

It was October 1, 2011. I wrote of God's affirmation after a phone conversation I had with Mom Bev. In speaking with her, she shared with me how Isaiah chapter 43 highlighted that I was precious and honorable and that the Lord loved me. I woke up the next morning and read the entire chapter of this Isaiah book. Isaiah 43 verse 19 spoke clearly to me, *"God is about to make a way in the wilderness and rivers in the Desert."* It was as if God was speaking to me directly and then reaffirmed the same message to me through a sermon that was preached that weekend at church by Pastor Christy. "I will do a new thing **in** you!" That day in my journal as I fed more of God's words I wrote:

God is about to bring me to my destination, my breakthrough! Hallelujah! "So do not throw away your confidence; it will be richly rewarded. You need to persevere so that when you have done the will of God, you will receive what he has promised," Hebrews 10:35–36 (NIV). "… but the righteous person will live by his faithfulness," Habakkuk 2:4 (NIV).

I was overwhelmed by the feeling that I was on the brink of something amazing. I was reminded of God's encouragement written in Malachi 3:3 that I rewrote in my journal that October. It shared how a silversmith holds the silver in the midst of the fire to purify it and knows it is refined and perfect when he sees his reflection in it. God knows I had definitely felt like I had been through the fire in this journey. I came to realize this was part of the faith purification process God needed me to endure. I had begun to see His reflection in my journey. I wrote, thank you God for being my silversmith!

As I grew closer to God, He reminded me that the vision He allowed me to see in February 2007 was still real, even though I had removed myself mentally and physically from the process. Long before I ever encountered conversations of IVF or failed fertility treatments, miscarriages, endometritis, talks of surrogacy, and all the stuff of the past several years, His promise to me would still be fulfilled.

October 2011 was truly a pivotal turning point for me. My journal writing had evolved. While visiting Mom Bev in Maryland, she reminded me of the importance of recording times and dates the Holy Spirit brings to us. She said this adds to the importance of recognizing that God alone should receive the glory when the dates, times, and actions that we were directed to write occurs. She shared with me her personal story of how she had written in her Bible on March 8, 2009 that young men would flock to God. That same weekend in October 2011 while visiting with Mom Bev, 113 people were baptized at her church and the majority of them were young men.

When I left Maryland, I sat on a very small plane, and as it noisily began to ascend through the clouds, I pulled out my brown journal. Honestly, I was feeling nervous as to what I was about to write. My mind began to process the likely possibility of 'what if' someday I had children who would read the words that I wrote, my words regarding the vision that God gave me years earlier in February 2007. The plane ascended further into the clouds, and I wrote:

It is only recently that I have shared this vision with a few others due to my challenges. This vision provides me hope and confidence that what God showed me and told me that morning that He will do it! At that point in 2007, I was not aware of the challenges or losses that would be ahead of me to cause me to lose sight or forget this vision. However, God has restored this vision now by placing "times" in my spirit of when things, no, rather, new life will be created. Lord, you know the flesh right now is thinking, and almost fearful as to what I am about to write. Because of what it thinks the Spirit will make me place on these pages for somewhat fear of embarrassment or doubt that it will come to pass, but I must write, I must write it down. So you alone Lord can receive the glory! Because only you alone can and will do it. By November 2012, thirteen months from now, you will do it! As I pause and write again, you will bless Dwayne and I with a child from my womb that will lift your name on High!

To wrap up 2011, Hubby and I made the once-in-a-lifetime trip on New Year's Eve to New York City to watch the infamous ball drop. We joined one of my closest childhood friends and her husband. They also had not been able to have kids after several years of marriage, but we both never stopped believing that someday we would be parents. For now, we were living and loving our best life in the cold Big Apple. We had an amazing, exhilarating, and absolutely fun time! The night was cold, very cold and we had walked many blocks in New York City to actually get a glimpse of the ball. In that moment as the countdown began, my husband held me as tight as he could in my bulky winter jacket. We squeezed tightly to each other in the large crowd, we yelled, "3, 2, 1… Happy New Year," and secretly I made my wish!

Yes, I made my wish to have a baby. We kissed, laughed, snapped pictures, and shouted Happy New Year several more times along with all the New Year's Eve revelers. With blinking neon 2012 New Year's glasses, we were in full celebration mode. There was so much excitement and I felt there was indeed so much to look forward to. I was at peace, I was excited, I was happy, and I felt that whatever God was about to do next in my life, I was satisfied. Satisfied!

Yes, that's where I was stepping into 2012, happy, excited, filled up on God, at peace, and satisfied. I was reminded of my grandmother's final two words to me before she died, "Be Satisfied." For me, I knew she did not mean to be complacent with life, since she was a woman who was always striving and believed in God's power to achieve anything. But I knew she meant for me to always be content and at peace. I felt she would be pretty proud of me and smile if she realized how I had truly embraced being in a satisfied state, content, and at peace. I was living my *Faith INfertilty.*

Chapter 10

BUY BABY BLANKETS

❝ *To obey is better than sacrifice, and to heed is better than the fat of rams," 1 Samuel 15:22 (NIV).*

❝ *You're blessed when you stay on course, walking steadily on the road revealed by God. You're blessed when you follow his directions, doing your best to find him. That's right – you don't go off on your own; you walk straight along the road he set. You, God, prescribed the right way to live; now you expect us to live it. Oh, that my steps might be steady, keeping to the course you set; Then I'd never have any regrets in comparing my life with your counsel," Psalm 110:1-8 (MSG).*

It was time! January 2012, we made the decision that we were ready to try again. During our hiatus from trying to have a baby, I felt my relationship with God grow deeper, and I began to distinctly hear Him speaking to me in various ways.

Shortly after deciding to try again this time I heard God speak to me and directing me to do something that seemed absolutely absurd - buy baby blankets. *What?* I thought. *Buy baby blankets? But I don't have a baby.* And oddly enough, nobody I knew at the time was expecting. But the direction was clear! Buy baby blankets! It was also clear that this direction was for no one else, but my baby. I called my sister-in-law the next morning after I had received the spiritual direction. I told her how crazy it seemed but that I was going to purchase a few baby blankets for my future baby that I felt God was impressing on me to purchase them . I remember her clearly telling me, "Girl you better listen to God!" And we both laughed. Later that month, I had a business trip to Maryland and visited my Mom Bev and provided her the first of the four blankets that I had purchased. I shared with her that God was directing me to deliver these blankets in person for my mothers to pray over the life that will be held in the blankets. It was not until the last few moments before I was to leave that I gave her the blanket because I felt the idea of what I was about to do almost seemed silly. I was about to leave. We were standing in her driveway when I told her. She gladly accepted the assignment and hugged me. Mom Bev told me that she was honored to be part of God's interesting assignment and that she would be praying over the blanket every day.

My next trip took me to Fort Lauderdale to my Mom Tonya. She was my graduate school mom who fed me and fed me and fed me lots of good native Bahamian food. Again, I repeated the assignment from God to provide a blanket to pray over the future baby that will be held in it. She was my warfare Wednesday praying mom, but let me know this assignment would be an every weekday warfare prayer! The next blanket was delivered to Ms. Joni, who also had accepted me as one of her own children when my husband and I relocated to Central Florida. She had been there many times to comfort and pray for me after the loss of my twins. She was one of a few persons who was aware of the loss of my baby angel. She was one who stood in the gap in prayer for me when I could not pray for myself. Ms. Joni accepted the assignment of the baby blanket. The final baby blanket was delivered in person to my mom in the Bahamas, February 2012. I let her know that it will someday hold her grandchild. I know she would be a great praying grandmother, and her assignment began now. Lord that was wild, but I did it. Sometimes we have to step out on faith and actualize the very thing that we have been praying for.

My faith was activated and being actualized INfertility with these blankets.

The beginning of 2012 began with my eyes seeing God's hand move in impossible matters. I was engaged in the prayers of finding a missing child, the release of a friend's son who was detained unfairly, and the manifestation of my childhood friend I spent the New Year with becoming pregnant. After years of being told that she may not be able to have a baby, and starting the year with a baby wish just like me in NYC, she now had her miracle in her womb! The missing child was found safe, and my friend's son was finally home. I was excited, and just amazed at God's miraculous power in these impossible matters!

March 2012, I was on a business trip, this time to Denver, Colorado. We had just decided to proceed with IVF again at the start of the year. God's direction was clear, and I was at peace. We had enjoyed our break; we were refreshed and ready to move forward and I had just completed God's incredibly odd assignment with buying baby blankets.

Coincidently, as we began the next IVF cycle the required initial baseline scans and checks coincided with this business trip. I was going to be away from home for the next 2 weeks between Colorado and Maryland. Okay Lord should I wait? The song from Fred Hammond, "We Are More Than Able," then began to replay in my head as a reminder that we did not need to delay because we were more than able to press on now. Without much hoopla, a clinic was found in the Denver area that was able to seamlessly accommodate me and have my information sent to my doctors in Florida. As I sat in my hotel room that day, I wrote the following in my journal with a heart full of gratitude and anticipation:

> *God nothing is impossible with you! We just thank you! You are a God of miracles! So, today I begin my other journey to see your miracle of life manifested in me. Despite my results last week of the return of endometritis, I am still thanking you for what you are going to do in me, and that anything that the enemy wishes to bring against me will be destroyed by my God's power! Glory to God in the highest! Now Lord I commit this day, week, month, and year in this very hour of my entire life and each extension of it fully to you.*

God's specialty in impossible matters and receiving His blessings now became evident. However, clearly the enemy was not pleased with the season I was in spiritually as he began to devise ways to discourage me. We were now in the midst of a fresh IVF cycle, and I began to encounter surprisingly new unforeseen challenges at work, and even more surprising challenges within my marriage. This was frustrating after such a great break from fertility treatment, baby talk, and actively pursuing my motherhood dreams. Now, after all that here I was trying to conceive again and two areas of my life that were reasonably good and stable were unwinding. My practice of writing in my journal had brought me to a new era of reflection and recalibration that was greatly needed now. I realized it was important for me to write in my journal my challenges along with my blessings. It was important for me to note that God was still God in the midst of the good and bad times and in the midst of all our troubles! On April 12, 2012, I wrote in my journal:

> *I had come to the other side of the spiritual warfare I know has been raging to discourage my soul, I'm grateful that you O God, have brought me over. Thank you, God for opening my spiritual eyes and showing me how the strategic attacks were set to break me. And then further bring discord in me and my husband's communication. I thank you again for affirming the battles of this life are not my own. And then to know a member of my team speaks false allegations against me. Thank you, God, for the peace, your peace that could only come from you in the midst of it all.*

> *There is a saying that it is always darkest before the dawn... and I am able to write confidently that over all these things, victory is mine! The Dawn is about to break and tonight Lord as I lay me down to sleep I say for these trials – thank you for the storm and thank you for the 'big blessing' on the way.*

> *I'm Pregnant!*

Chapter 11

MY RAINBOW BABY

" *And my God will meet all your needs according to the riches of his glory in Christ Jesus,"* **Philippians 4:19 (NIV).**

What's in a rainbow? Beautiful colors, joy, happiness, and love that always come after the rain. I was a mother in waiting, secretly standing in the rain that seemed to never end. Yet the vision God shared with me in prior years, kept reminding me to holdfast, as the rain would soon end and my rainbow was on the way.

My Dollar Store pregnancy test, my OneStep name brand test, the beta blood pregnancy test, ultrasound 1, and ultrasound 2 were all complete, it was official as official could possibly be, I was indeed pregnant and carrying one beautiful little baby inside my womb. At this time, I was still cautiously optimistic that this was it. I can still remember calling my mothers - to whom I had given the prayer blankets - and sharing my exciting news. Now more than ever, I truly needed them to continue praying over the blankets and the life I was carrying to be held in them. I didn't share the news of my pregnancy with anyone else outside of my mothers.

A healthy diet, no travel, no stress, no spotting. I walked gingerly wherever I went. Honestly, I still felt nervous about going to each doctor's appointment during my first trimester. The turbulence at work and in my marriage that occurred during my IVF cycle had settled. Everything was truly smooth sailing.

I crossed the first trimester! Hallelujah, thank you, Jesus! I was not able to keep my secret much longer at work, as not only was I beginning to show, but I had declined to join in upcoming work-related travel.

My amazing perinatologist, a.k.a. high-risk prenatal doctor, had recommended additional safety precautions given my history, including having a cerclage. While it was not a procedure I looked forward to having, I was willing to do whatever it took to save this baby. This included me getting a needle in my spine for a spinal tap for the cerclage procedure which essentially was having the neck of my cervix pulled forward and wrapped around tight several times with a string. Yes, ouch! While the procedure was not painful, it was uncomfortable as I could feel every pull and tug and twist that my doctor made to ensure that my cervix was sealed tight to prevent my baby from having the chance of slipping out.

It's a girl! I was in shock when the ultrasound technician said those words as I was confident I was pregnant with a little boy. Honestly, it did not matter whether we had a boy or a girl, we just wanted to have a successful pregnancy and deliver a healthy baby. It finally felt like my pregnancy was on cruise control, although as we approached the five-month mark I began to think of my twins. It had been three years since I delivered my twins in Ohio. But this time was different, no twins, no fibroids, no bleeding, Lord we are finally on our victory lap!

How did we finally get here? At my last appointment my doctor was suggesting surrogacy, and prior to that we didn't know how we could afford IVF. Anyone who has ever inquired about the cost of fertility treatment knows it is not cheap as repeated doctor visits, almost daily blood tests, ultrasounds, and other examinations come with an expensive price tag.

I recall the first time my husband and I went to the doctor to explore the option of fertility treatment. At that time it averaged around $10-$12,000 per cycle. My health insurance did not include IVF treatment plans and none of the pre-work-up related to receiving future fertility treatment. As a young couple, we did okay financially, but we did not have insurance plans that would cover fertility treatments, and neither did we have $10,000 saved in the bank. How was this even going to be remotely possible? But, God!!!

We had multiple failed IVF attempts, yet we never took out a loan, nor did we receive an inheritance, or have a rich benefactor. But what we did have was a very real God. A few months after exploring IVF treatment plans, my employer was acquired by another company that was based in another state. This new state that I was now technically employed under required its employers to provide insurance plans that included family planning options inclusive of fertility treatments. My new insurance plan not only included IVF, but it allowed for up to six attempts with minimal co-payment and zero payments for all labs and pre-work-up expenses associated with IVF. As I continuously reflect over this entire experience it is indeed mind boggling to see how God's hand was at work orchestrating this from the very beginning. And yes, God knew that we would need all six attempts available in the insurance plan so that there would be no question in our minds of His hand moving on our behalf in His time! Jesus had paid it all!

I was falling in love with my daughter! After very little debate, my husband and I named our daughter Jasmine. During our evening walks with our dog, there was an area in our neighborhood where the amazing smell of jasmine flowers would mesmerize us before we saw it. Each Sunday, Jasmine and I began the ritual of sitting on the couch reading baby books while she was in my womb. I was still at peace, I was still content, and I was satisfied at 22 weeks pregnant.

I had developed cravings for Chipotle and pizza while pregnant, which Jasmine and I feasted on frequently. However, just as I finished up my pizza dinner one night, extreme nausea began to settle in. During my entire pregnancy to this point I did not have any significant morning sickness symptoms, yet here I was extremely nauseated. Was it my dinner? I was not holding anything down. I called my doctor's office who provided me with recommendations of what to safely take. Nothing was working. My husband was at work and I was home alone. I quickly went from nausea, to vomiting, to pain.

What was happening? To this day, I still do not recall how I got to the hospital, but I do remember that I was in extreme pain. My faith was once again on the frontlines. To this point, other than the pain medication that I was given after my cerclage procedure, I had not even taken a pain pill, yet I was screaming for some type of medication to relieve the pain while keeping my baby safe. I remember the nurse saying they had to wait to give me any medication until it was confirmed that I was not in labor and rule out other causes for the pain.

Surprisingly, fear had not set in which I believe was in part because of the intensity of the pain I was in, but mostly because my faith in this season was different and had been fortified. While I had been down this road before, I was not going to just roll over without a spiritual fight and using my weapon of faith and prayer over my daughter's life. The doctors were not able to confirm the source of my pain, but they were able to confirm that I was not in labor and my beautiful daughter was doing okay.

The moment the doctors gave the green light for my nurses to provide me with morphine and the pain reliever hit my IV line, my new friend Morphe, (my nickname for morphine), became my new BFF as the pain almost immediately went away within a minute or two. With the exception of having elevated amylase and lipase levels, everything checked out fine. I was discharged after about five days when my pain had finally subsided without medication.

A baby that is born after the pain of infertility and loss is referred to as a rainbow baby; a reflection of beauty and joy after the rain. My journey to having my rainbow baby was anything but a rainbow experience. The enemy was not through with me yet and this was just the beginning of the fight for my daughter's life and for me maintaining my sanity. A week later I was readmitted to the hospital with the same excruciating pain and all I wanted was to meet up with my BFF Morphe once again. I remember crying to the admitting nurse, "I know what this is, I was just here last week please let me see my buddy Morphe." Fortunately or unfortunately, I had to wait; wait to be evaluated, wait for lab tests to return, and wait for the doctors to give clearance for me and Morphe to be friends again.

At this point, I felt I knew the drill, they would patch me up, my pain would be relieved, and I would go home within five days. My faith was not letting up. My five days turned into two weeks. The two-week period was a myriad of issues out of a pregnant woman's nightmare. There was poking, prodding, whole-body machine MRI tests, being wheeled in a gurney from one floor to another. So much was happening. I was still vomiting most days, and doctors went from a possible diagnosis of gall stones to pancreatitis. I was concerned as to what all these tests would mean for my precious Jasmine, given my exposure to so many tests.

Here I was in the hospital, where I went from thinking I would be patched up and sent home within a few days to being told I needed surgery and eventually being hooked up to a TPN (feeding line) inserted in my right arm. My amylase and lipase level had also fluctuated so badly during this hospital stay that I was labeled NPO; a medical term that essentially meant I was not allowed to put anything in my mouth, I was not allowed to eat for almost two weeks. When I did resume with liquids, it took me 2 1/2 days to drink just a half-size can of ginger ale. In all transparency, it was downright miserable, and I was extremely uncomfortable.

I eventually settled into the fact that I was not going to let these tests or food distract me from the assignment of saving my baby. I was in spiritual and physical warfare.

While I knew within my heart that I had not done anything wrong that brought me to this point, there were those weird moments when the enemy sent me discouraging thoughts that made me wonder about my choice for IVF. Self-doubt is a vice. The enemy would very craftily have my mind ponder on if this path of fertility choice was what God had for me and if I was once again dealing with the consequences. Crazy right? Thankfully, however, the peace and spirit of God quickly extinguished those thoughts by reminding me that *"Every good and perfect gift is from above, coming down from the Father of the heavenly lights,"* James 1:17 (NIV). Certainly, my Jasmine was a good, perfect, and beautiful gift created by Him.

I was on my 14th day of being in the hospital and signs of my health improvement were evident. I had finally begun eating solids again and had two days of keeping them down. My doctor came in early on Day 14 and told me that given my progress there was a chance I would be discharged. It was a Friday morning and I was beyond excited at the thought of finally spending the weekend in my own bed. I was told that three tests were necessary and if they all came back good, I would be discharged. The nurses were told to begin the paperwork for follow-up, at-home healthcare for the TPN line that was still inserted in my arm and wound care if it was removed before I was discharged. I was super excited and began to call my parents and a few friends to let them know I was heading home likely later that evening. I was giddy with thoughts of seeing my dog again and finishing preparations at home to welcome Jasmine in a few months.

My bed was directly facing a clock above the bathroom door in my hospital room. It was exactly 4:43 p.m. that Friday afternoon when my doctor finally came back. With a sheepish smile, he quickly cleared his throat and read my first two test results that were great, but then shared that my third test result was not the best and therefore I would be staying there until I delivered my baby. Wait, what? That was at least another nine weeks away! Are you sure? How? Why? I desperately wanted to go home.

As the doctor stood there explaining my test results, for all of about five minutes I began to soak my emotional wounds in pity water. I was just all in my feelings. I then realized here I was again! The enemy was not letting up in trying to crush my spirit. However, the foundation of my faith and recognizing how far God had brought me, snatched me back into the reality of how blessed I was. Despite having spent a total of already three weeks in the hospital from my prior and current hospital stay, and now being told I could be here for up to another nine weeks was disheartening, to say the least. Regardless my mindset shifted as it came to settle in the thoughts of recognizing I was in one of the best hospital facilities, my husband worked in the same hospital two floors above me, and technically I would be getting room service every day for the next nine weeks. That evening I wrote in my journal,

> *I am about to show the enemy these next few weeks that he picked the wrong one to deter from celebrating her blessings! All the blessings of today, my TPN bag was removed! I am free from the IV pole! Jasmine is 2 lbs., 6 oz. right where she should be at this stage! It has been five days since I last vomited or had excruciating pain, and it has been two days since I have been able to keep down solid food.*

As news started to reach family and friends that I was going to be hospitalized for the next nine weeks, I made it clear that no one was to have pity on me or my situation because I never wanted to give way to the enemy believing that he had won this fight!

I recognize that the enemy does not fight fair, and my strongest weapon against him was my faith. Therefore it was necessary for my faith to be guarded against self-pity or the pity of others during this time.

The next nine weeks were filled with many high and few low moments. Daily, I would have a fetal heartbeat monitor strapped around my waist each morning and evening. Every Sunday I would be placed on a scale where the needle never seemed to move to the weight levels my doctors wanted from me. I never quite got used to the 'nutritional' drink supplements required with each meal to help with my weight gain. However, these were minor inconveniences as I was tended to by the best healthcare team of nurses, doctors, and technicians. The smiles of the cleaning ladies who became my friends that I talked to each day were an unexpected treat, and I was able to work full-time from my hospital bed meeting the needs of my team on a daily basis.

Little did I realize at the start of this hospital stay how blessed my experience would be. Not only did I make amazing friends with various members of the hospital staff who became like my family during this time, but I was also blessed with two amazing baby showers hosted by my work colleagues and my church family respectively.

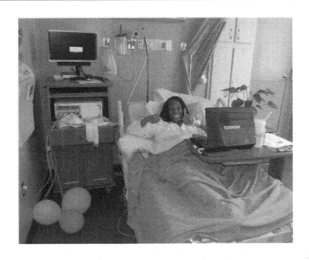

Working full-time from my hospital bed where I spent over 75 days on bedrest. Discharged finally when I reached 34 weeks of pregnancy.

Before this hospital stay was over, before I would meet my beautiful rainbow baby, the enemy had one more very nasty trick up his sleeve. It was the day of my baby shower and I was on top of the world with the expectations of joy and love to be shared with my family and friends. Then, the enemy, always ready to steal my joy, started with me being awoken by Dr. "X." She shared the news that she suspected there may be a mild borderline birth defect with my baby due to her recent findings from an ultrasound I had the day before. There was extra fluid around my daughter's brain. Dr. X stated that I may have been exposed to a particular virus which is one of the causes of this particular birth defect. She wanted to test my blood to determine if I had been exposed to it during the last 6 to 12 months. She shared that if I was exposed to the virus my baby could be deaf, blind, or have some other form of learning disability. The doctor wanted to order a highly advanced MRI test that would require the MRI department of the hospital to actually reset their machines specifically for my test. I wrote in my journal that day:

The devil is a liar and God reigns supreme! No weapon formed against me or my child shall prosper! She shall be born healthy, strong, without issues and will be a living testimony that brings honor and glory only to God! The Lord reminded me of the song, "I Know The Plans I Have For You" by Martha Munizzi. He also reminded me of his word in Jeremiah 29:11, "He knows the plan he has for me, to give me hope, joy, and strength for everything I go through! Plans to prosper, and keep in good health all that he has promised!"

After being encouraged by God's promise in word and song I tried to reach my husband to talk for a while but got no answer after a few attempts. Within a few moments, he called me back and my ringtone for his calls was that song – I Know The Plans I Have For You. In that moment, it hit me what God had just done. So distinctly, through such a simple measure of a ringtone He reaffirmed His plans, His promise, and His love for me. I was tickled with joy and exceeding love for my Master and I was ready to celebrate His goodness at my baby shower.

Through God's unmerited favor, I successfully reached the golden number of 34 weeks! My daughter Jasmine was still thriving inside of me, I felt great. Unbelievably I was being kicked out of the hospital to spend the rest of my time at home. My doctors said that at this point regardless of whether I went into labor now they would not delay my delivery. It was hospital policy I was told given at 34 weeks a baby is able to suck and swallow on their own. It was all very surreal; I was off of hospital bed rest and heading home. It was November 30, I had just crossed over the 37-week mark and at my high-risk doctor visit, she said it was time. Yes, it was November! Just as I had written in my journal on that small plane a year ago. November was the month that my daughter was given the eviction paper notice that she was ready to be delivered. The C-Section was scheduled for the following week.

My beautiful rainbow daughter and happy joyous flower Jasmine was born at 6 lbs., with no birth defects. The evidence of my *Faith INfertilty* was alive, breathing, and nestled in my bosom. My rainbow baby, Jasmine had arrived.

Chapter 12

TWINS AGAIN??

> ❝ *He does our praying in and for us, making prayer out of our wordless sighs, our aching groans. He knows us far better than we know ourselves, knows our pregnant condition, and keeps us present before God. That's why we can be so sure that every detail in our lives of love for God is worked into something good,"* Romans 8:26-28 (MSG).

The levels of self-doubt and self-questioning that I had when going through the IVF process challenged my faith, God's will for my life, and the foundation of my relationship with Him.

My husband and I were in awe every day for the gift of life in Jasmine that God had blessed us with after the journey we had been on for so many years. She was definitely worth the wait and everything we endured. The love and joy we experienced in bringing Jasmine home could never fully be described on these pages. She is truly smart, beautiful, and amazing! We know now that God orchestrated the design of her life through the journey that we encountered. Just before she was born, my praying mothers sent us the prayer blankets I gave them. Jasmine was wrapped in the blankets and our church minister prayed for us before we were discharged from the hospital. Jasmine's baby dedication was held during a special service exactly one year from the date I had given the first blanket to Mom Bev. God's timing and sense of humor were very clear.

Jasmine is held on her baby dedication day by her praying mothers who each had a baby blanket they prayed over in faith before she was ever conceived. All blankets were stitched together by her grandma Rose.

Fast-forward two years later. We made the decision to grow our family further and used two remaining frozen embryos from our cycle with Jasmine. I distinctly remember the doctor asking if we wanted to use one or two? He also advised that with frozen embryos, inserting a second one typically helps the first embryo to implant better and can result in just a single pregnancy. My husband held my hand, looked at the doctor, and said, "We'll take the two." I quickly pulled my hand away from him and sitting up on the stretcher asked him, "Are you sure? What if we end up with twins again? What if my pregnancy outcome has similar challenges as the first time when we lost Azaria and DJ? What if we do give birth to two babies? How are we going to manage with three little kids?"

He looked at me and sheepishly smiled, "We are going to do the two embryos, everything will be fine, and God is the only one who will decide." I laid back down took a deep breath and stared at the ceiling that had pictures of marine animals covering the fluorescent lights. My fertility doctor then told us a short story that his wife had twin boys via a frozen embryo transfer, and that they were now amazing young men in the world. Then he asked, "What's the final verdict?" I closed my eyes, whispered a prayer, and then held up two fingers.

Two sacs, two heartbeats! Everything looks great. Each doctor visit went smoothly. My high-risk prenatal doctor said it was as if I had a classic textbook pregnancy for twins, everything was going so smoothly. Even the cerclage surgical procedure, although uncomfortable, was still much better this time around. The scale at the doctor's office however was never my friend, as it always told the tale that I was not gaining enough weight despite my attempt to eat around the clock. Regardless, my doctors were pleased overall with my pregnancy.

While our faith was grounded that this would end positively we had several moments of just being cautiously optimistic.

I was directed by my friends to get the genders placed in a sealed envelope during my gender ultrasound for a gender reveal party. The gender was not revealed to me at that ultrasound, but deep within my heart, I believed I was going to have a boy and a girl just like in my first pregnancy. Fast forward to the second half of my gender reveal party. "Sugar and spice and all that's nice. But wait that's my big sister Jasmine! Just like my brother baby #1, I'm a boy #2!" What? Two boys! As the poem was read and a second blue baby jersey was opened in the gender reveal package, I was stunned with laughter. Two boys!

We had moved from our two-bedroom condo to a larger home, Jasmine was reading and potty trained, and I had started a dream job working from home. My pregnancy was progressing great with many measures in place to avoid some of the challenges I had the first time. The Lord's Word was being manifested in my life in a profound way. I was grateful. I was happy. But, it is in moments like this that we must never forget, the enemy never sleeps.

It was March 2015, after much debate in the doctor's office my husband provided the scheduled C-section date. He wanted them born as close to his birthday as possible, and I wanted them born on another date because I wanted a specific doctor, and he was not available for the date my husband wanted. So my choice was to either give my husband his birthday wish or go with the doctor that I wanted. For the moment, he got his wish.

Despite the perfect textbook pregnancy, despite having a scheduled c-section date, at 31 weeks with great dismay, my water broke. Dear God, No! Not now, not yet. It was too early.

The rarity of how everything unfolded when this happened proves to me that God is still present in even the most difficult and challenging circumstances. My brother and sister-in-law who lived in Memphis, Tennessee had flown into Tampa about an hour and a half away from our home. Their flight was delayed coming to Florida, and despite being tired and exhausted when they arrived, they made the decision to drive to our home versus checking into the nearby hotel where they had originally planned to stay. They arrived at our home around 3 a.m. Their presence that night was a pleasant surprise as I had not expected them until the next day. My husband was at work at the hospital that night, and Jasmine and I had curled up for the night in my bed. They made themselves comfortable and went to bed.

It was exactly two hours later that my water broke. I am absolutely certain that God planned this provision in advance for me, as my brother-in-law, Jay, was able to drive me to the hospital while my sister-in-law, Noreen, stayed home to watch Jasmine.

My husband met us in the driveway of the hospital with a wheelchair anxiously waiting to wheel me in. I had called my mom, so she and her prayer warriors would pray for me. I asked them to please pray for the safety of my babies to stay tucked inside me until it was time for them to be born. I was too early.

Once more, I had to let my faith be bigger than my fears and serve the enemy notice that he had picked the wrong one again. As the nurses and doctors started to tend to me, they confirmed that I had broken my amniotic sac and that I indeed had begun premature labor. Flashbacks of my first twins' deliveries came to me briefly. I began to plea, "Please save my babies. Please do whatever it takes to stop me from going into full labor." My doctors and nurses did just that as they hooked me up to many IV lines, and also provided me with oxygen. I told them I had been here before and had stayed over eleven weeks with my daughter. I was prepared to stay for another six weeks if that's what it took to keep my babies baking inside until it was time to be delivered. I knew the nurses, I knew the doctors, I even knew the cleaning crew, I knew this place. I just needed them to stop me from going into labor and I would settle in and be fine here for the next few weeks.

It was early Saturday morning when I was admitted, and by mid-afternoon I was really feeling the contractions. Each contraction felt like a wrestle with the enemy. I was given magnesium to help my babies' lungs strengthen should I deliver them. Do what is necessary, I told my nurses, but I'm not giving up. As I prayed, and felt the prayers of others praying for me, I could feel the lessening of the contractions. God and medicine worked wonders on me that day! By early evening, my contractions had stopped. My boys were still quite active inside of me, I was good. Thank you, Jesus!

I remember calling my mom in the Bahamas to let her know not to be concerned about traveling now, and that I would see her in a few weeks. I was good now. My son's godmothers Penny and June came to the hospital that Saturday when they heard I had gone into labor. As my husband had just worked a 12-hour shift at the hospital, they sent him home to rest and I was at peace knowing Jasmine was safe with her aunt and cool young cousin, Lexia. Penny and June, like angels, stayed by my hospital bedside as I drifted in and out of sleep.

By Sunday morning, the flurry of activities had settled down. I was feeling good. I tried to reach my mom in the Bahamas when I woke up only to discover that she was already in Miami about to board a connecting flight to get to me. This woman, my mother you gave me Lord, I sighed. By noon my mom was by my side and she relieved Pat and Joey. I will admit that I did fuss at my mom for not waiting until I told her she needed to come. However, I was secretly ecstatic to see her and beyond happy to have my mommy by my side.

By Sunday afternoon, my high-risk prenatal doctor came to visit me and told me she needed to remove my cerclage. It had been over 24 hours since I was admitted and although my contractions had ended, she noted if they started again, and I had fast labor activity I was at risk of having my cervix being torn and potentially hemorrhaging internally. While I didn't want to risk personal injury I also did not want to prepare for an early delivery. I believed I was not going into labor. I refused to let her remove it. I felt it was probably what was keeping my babies from slipping out. I did not have a cerclage with my first set of twins and they just slid away from me in the delivery room. I rationalized with my doctor that I had a c-section scheduled in a few weeks. Despite these many answers I had for my doctor, she was firm and told me she was not going to risk my bleeding to death. And while there was a greater risk of me still going into premature labor she was not going to risk me hemorrhaging by keeping the cerclage in.

To this point, I had been lying on my side with my legs closed as tight as possible. I was not letting these babies out. I kept hearing the magic number was 34 weeks, Lord let me get to 34 weeks, please. I don't know what all happened down there when the cerclage was being removed, but all I remember seeing was a sterile silver pan being taken away with something covered in blood. My doctor then encouraged me to relax but let me know my body will do what it wants to do when it was ready, but at least there won't be a risk of me hemorrhaging. After all the tugging and pulling to remove the cerclage, surprisingly I still felt fine.

My in-laws, husband, and mom were all there visiting with me that Sunday afternoon. I felt the need to rest, and I knew my husband needed to go to work later that night. I told everyone to go home and hugged my in-laws goodbye as I knew they also needed to make their return back to Tampa to complete the purpose of their trip before returning to Tennessee. It was about 5:00 p.m., and as they all left, I began to eat my dinner and relax. A few minutes later, my mom returned and said she told the others to go home and that she would stay with me. I told her it was not necessary, but I was glad to have some alone time with her.

As I finished my dinner and began to relax, one of my obstetrician (OB) doctors came in to evaluate me. After she had prodded me several times, she looked up and asked where my husband was. I let her know that I had sent him home as he needed to prepare for his work shift that began at 7:00 p.m. that night. She then looked at me in a matter-of-fact style and said you need to call him to come back now, your cervix is almost nonexistent, and we are taking you to deliver your babies now. I was in shock.

My mom was by my side, as I called for my husband to come back to the hospital. There was a flurry of activity that once more swirled around me. Meds were being placed in my IV, calls were being made, and I was being shaved down below. I could barely get my thoughts together as everything was moving so quickly. The only thing I had within me to say was Jesus please keep me safe, please keep my boys safe. They began to wheel me to the operating room, and I remember crying, "please wait for my husband I'm sure he's almost here." The whirlwind of activity continued in the operating room. The NICU doctor started to rattle off what would happen with my babies, the anesthesiologist began to explain the spinal tap procedure that I was very familiar with and positioned me for the needle they were about to place in my back. As they were speaking, to my relief my husband entered the operating room. He squeezed my hands.

I was positioned on the table. With my stomach hidden behind the blue hanging tarp, I began to feel the tugging and pulling on my stomach. Then, the first cry, it's a boy. More tugging, more pulling, we're breech my doctor shouted. More tugging, more pulling. It felt as if something tied to me would not let loose as they continued to pull and then the release. There was no cry, no sound and my heart raced wondering if my second son was okay. I didn't get to see either of my babies when they were delivered as they placed them through an open window directly behind the curtain that was connected to the NICU.

About an hour later after I had been closed up, I was being wheeled back to my room when the nurse said let's take her stretcher through the NICU to see her boys. I sat up on the stretcher and got the first peek of my beautiful sons.

At thirty-one weeks, my miracles were thriving as if they were much older. With Andre, my baby #1, not needing oxygen and baby number two, my Alex, only staying on oxygen for the next five days. They were very tiny miracles who had other highs and lows while staying in the NICU for the next six weeks. I was blessed with two strong, healthy, amazing, and rambunctious boys at a new intersection of my *Faith INfertility* journey.

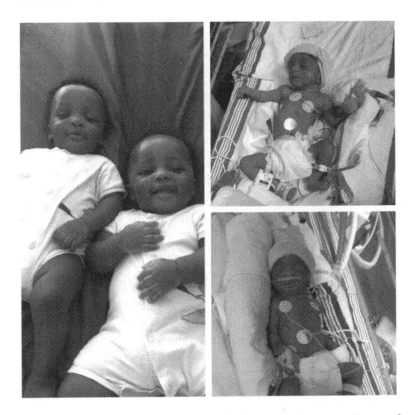

Twins, Alex and André, were delivered at 31weeks and spent several weeks in the neonatal intensive care unit (NICU). Despite André having to get surgery a month later for other health challenges, both boys have grown up as healthy rambunctious kids. Picture on right was a few hours after birth and picture on left is the boys at six months old.

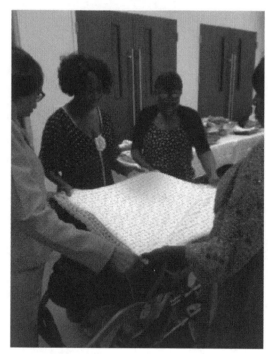

Prayer baby blankets were held over twins in their baby carriage on their baby dedication day by their praying mothers once more.

Chapter 13

RELEASING THE BURDEN & EXTINGUISHING THE SHAME

" *And he said to me, 'My grace is sufficient for you, for my power is made perfect in weakness ... Therefore I will boast all the more gladly about my weaknesses, so that Christ's power may rest on me,'"*
2 Corinthians 12:9 (NIV).

There was agony in the underlying discomfort of sharing the embarrassment and shame for something I had no control over.

Despite all the challenges and secrets of infertility, miscarriage, and heartache, this pain was eventually replaced with unspeakable joy and love that came with the birth of my daughter and my twin sons. I was excited, I was happy, I was grateful, joyful, and truly content, but yet somewhere in the recesses of my mind, I was still embarrassed.

Now that may sound like an oxymoron, and it is only now I realize that it was the plan of the enemy to make me feel this way. Let's not be mistaken, the enemy knows God has a purpose and a plan to fulfill His work in and through you and through your future generations. And unfortunately, the enemy will stop at nothing to fulfill his desire to thwart God's plan, by all means, necessary, including me feeling embarrassed and questioning if it is even Christian to pursue the use of fertility treatment.

As I pondered on how different I may have felt conceiving my children using 'traditional' methods, here's the most beautiful part of God's message to me. God reminded me that His ways are not my ways, His thoughts are not my thoughts, and that He has more than 1,000 ways to solve any situation of which we don't know even one.

Through God's message to me, I've come to realize in this experience, that the crafty trick the enemy had played on me has been played on many other women who have walked in my shoes. Women who have sat in the church pew next to a family with kids. Women who attended a birthday party and hear the squeal of children's laughter. Women who just walked outside their home and see their neighbor's kids dressed for school getting in the parent's car. Women, who like me, have silently wailed inside, "Lord, have you forgotten me?"

Many couples have secretly experienced countless tears and heartbreak of infertility. Unfortunately, they have not realized that it is a horrible trick of the enemy being played on Christian couples to not contemplate all their fertility options. If this is your struggle, remember this; regardless of medical intervention, God is the only creator of life! And all good and perfect gifts are from God!

We know the spiritual songs and we know the scriptures. Songs and scriptures that say, "My God is Bigger," "No weapon formed against me shall prosper," "I can do all things through Christ who gives me strength," and the list goes on. Make no mistake, my God IS BIGGER, I CAN do all things through Christ who gives me strength, and NO WEAPON formed against me shall prosper, especially not the weapon of infertility, shame, and deceit from the enemy! Continue to proclaim these during your *Faith INfertility* journey!

I've come to accept and realize it is time to expose the enemy's plan, free myself, and free others who question what actions the Holy Spirit has placed on their hearts to follow.

> *"I'm telling you these things while I'm still living with you. The Friend, the Holy Spirit whom the Father will send at my request, will make everything plain to you. He will remind you of all the things I have told you. I'm leaving you well and whole. That's my parting gift to you. Peace. I don't leave you the way you're used to being left—feeling abandoned, bereft. So don't be upset. Don't be distraught," John 14:25–27 (MSG).*

Very often in the early years of parenting my kids, I became fearful of the perception others may have of me if they knew I had fertility treatment to conceive them. God is all-powerful, and capable of doing anything without the assistance of medical intervention. I believe this wholeheartedly with every fiber of my being. I have personally seen God's power manifested like this through the cancellation of a rare terminal heart disease that my husband was diagnosed with several years ago. I have also seen his healing power in the lives of many others. The Scriptures have certainly highlighted many stories of how God was able to restore people even to the extent of someone touching just the hem of His garment.

However, God has also used other resources to fulfill His promises to us including people, projects, and yes even modern medicine, to reveal Himself in a great way that we may not understand. On my last visit with my fertility doctor, before my daughter was conceived, I recall him pulling out a book and pieces of literature highlighting how sometimes despite all efforts a woman's womb is unable to carry a pregnancy to term. It was one of the most difficult visits I had as he concluded by suggesting it was time for me to consider surrogacy. I remember leaving the office and sitting in my car wondering how others would perceive someone else carrying my child. What would they think of me? What would they think of my husband? And more so, what would they think of my faith? This was the end of the road, this was the door that would not open, this was my impossible situation. And now, not even medical intervention by one of the most distinguished fertility doctors in my state was letting me know there was nothing further he could do to help my situation but offer the concept of surrogacy. While surrogacy is a viable option for many couples struggling with infertility, we believed God was guiding us in another direction despite what the doctor had shared. Our faith was being reactivated!

After processing and agonizing over what was shared about our inability to carry a successful pregnancy, my husband

and I prayed, and through the Holy Spirit our faith was reactivated. In spite of our doctor's advice, we decided to give IVF one more attempt. This was very confusing for our medical team, why would we spend more time trying to achieve the impossible. It was now even being described as impossible by the best infertility doctor in this area. It was indeed after being told by my infertility doctor that my best option was surrogacy, after reaching a dead end and multiple losses, and multiple failed IVF attempts, that God used the resources of "infertility medicine" to fulfill His promise to me. In the process, He allowed this experience to be a witness to others in medicine that it was not the medicine alone that allowed me to conceive and carry to term, but it was the miraculous power of the living God showing up and showing out through my *faith INfertility*. This was a win-win for God. For too long the enemy has tried to place a question mark on my actions directed by the Holy Spirit to follow. For too long the painful secrets of infertility and the silence of my faith struggles remained fearful in the shadows of infertility.

> *"For the Spirit God gave us does not make us timid, but gives us power, love and self-discipline," 2 Timothy 1:7 (NIV).*

Many women may have experienced more challenges with infertility or have increased knowledge on how to address infertility, miscarriage, or infant loss. Unfortunately, however, many remain silent due to the stigma it may carry or because of the lack of an outlet in their Christian community to discuss it. God wants us to acknowledge that even in these circumstances, He is the only Creator of life. He wants me to share what I know based on my experience.

Have *Faith, INfertility*! Know that on the other side of your experience of heartbreak, loss, tears, sorrow, and pain is your path to something beautiful and amazing! Your path may not look like others, it may not look like anything you imagined or dreamed on your road to parenting. But it is okay to explore your options knowing that God has given wisdom to man to aid in the gift of parenthood. It's not the doctors, or the fertility shots, or the insemination, or any earthly thing that will give you the gift of parenthood. Therefore there is no need to hide any longer behind the guilt of exploring modern medicine to aid your fertility journey. This is not a question of your faith in God. God is with you, even in the silence of your fragile faith. Proceeding with fertility treatment does not reflect that you have decreased your faith in God's power to fulfill your dream of becoming a parent. Instead, it is an activation of your faith in following God's word that, *"…faith without deeds is dead,"* James 2:26 (NIV).

Use your journey to boldly declare that, God alone would receive the glory through the gift of life He creates in you, for you. He alone is the sole Creator of life in His time! In His time, IN His way, IN His power, IN faith, IN fertility, IN favor He makes all things beautiful! Take a look at my journey, it took many years of trying to become pregnant on my timeline, with my ideal traditional view of how I believed God wanted me to become a parent. Yet there were multiple fertility treatment failures, multiple endometrial biopsies, multiple miscarriages, multiple prayers, but God! In His time, in His way, and in His power, He gave me beauty for my ashes with multiple kids, who are multi-talented and have multiplied the reflection of God's goodness and grace through their talents and their exuberant love for family and friends.

My daughter who is approaching her 10th birthday, and who was reading since she was 2 years old, is a talented young violinist, my 7-year-old twins; one a gifted pianist and the other is an athlete "without bones," based on his agility. God makes no mistakes! This is how God showed me His power after many years of wanting and waiting and then instructing me to be still and patient as He crafted and molded my faith through what felt like a burning fire at times:

> "... though now for a little while you may have had to suffer grief in all kinds of trials. These have come so that the proven genuineness of your faith—of greater worth than gold, which perishes even though refined by fire—may result in praise, glory and honor when Jesus Christ is revealed," 1 Peter 1:7 (NIV).

He was preparing me *INfertility* for the season of parenthood, which I believe only came to fruition after my faith in Him was tested and tried and proven through the evidence of my three amazing children. Through the works of my faith to pursue and attempt conception non-traditionally.

Our family miraculously grew by 4 feet (literally), against all odds. God restores and God makes all things beautiful in His time. Photo credit: i4Perfection Photography.

Chapter 14

GOD MAKES ALL THINGS BEAUTIFUL IN HIS TIME

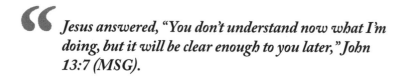

Jesus answered, "You don't understand now what I'm doing, but it will be clear enough to you later," John 13:7 (MSG).

In waiting, you are not forgotten but will be blessed in due season.

Finding the ability to persevere through life's disappointments and challenges has allowed my character to be refined and strengthened. Despite all the suffering and losses, God had given me the ability to endure patiently as He prepared me to receive His endless blessings of joy and love through His gift to me of my three amazing children. John Maxwell wrote, "Disappointment is the gap that exists between expectation and reality."[3] Unfortunately, my expectations of fertility had many gaps. Given the pain I experienced, how would I ever arrive at parenthood and even become a mother? Would holding a child of my own ever come to fruition? Then there was the gap between how people would perceive my infertility challenges or my journey to explore alternative fertility options. Would that reflect a lack of faith in God? The questions about these perceptions brought disappointment. I have chosen to no longer allow perceptions to block this story desperately needed by Christian women trying to conceive.

From countless, private one-on-one encounters of women secretly enduring the struggles of infertility and miscarriages, I have recognized the need to continuously birth encouragement and inspiration for others that they too can have the experience of God's restoration and *Faith INfertility*. In choosing to unveil my *Faith INfertility* journey, my faith has refined and strengthened my character to empower and encourage others on this journey. The unfortunate reality is that many individuals including friends, family, and yes even church folks may bring disappointments through their words

---

[3] Maxwell, J. C. (2011). *Put Your Dream to the Test: 10 Questions that Will Help You See it and Seize It*, p. 15, Thomas Nelson Inc.

or actions as you go through this journey. Recognize that others' responses to you on this journey may be uncomfortable and that their response may be due to a lack of knowledge and understanding of your experience.

However, it is valuable for the growth of your *Faith INfertility* to accept, learn, forgive, and still show love during these moments, first for yourself and then for others. These actions have allowed for my spiritual reflection and growth to continue as God pours His Holy Spirit in me and through me in my *Faith INfertility* journey. It is my prayer that this will also encourage and empower others.

While you wait and go through your *Faith INfertility* journey, remember God has not forgotten you. Your life is written on the palms of His hands. Just imagine how often you look at your hands each day and how often you use them. Your life is engraved on His hands.

> *"Can a mother forget the baby at her breast and have no compassion on the child she has borne? Though she may forget, I will not forget you! See, I have engraved you on the palms of my hands; your walls are ever before me," Isaiah 49:15-1 (NIV).*

Here God shares profoundly that even if a mother may forget her sucking child, He will never forget you!

I'll admit, waiting can be challenging, and woven with strings of discouragement. It was in January 2005 that my husband and I wrote our resolution and plans for becoming parents. We wrote the details of how we would share our baby announcement and our baby shower plans after a fabulous trip to Europe. We even had the baby room picked out. Yet, there were unknown years ahead of trying naturally, infertility treatments, biopsies, miscarriages, various diagnoses, and finally being told I would likely not be able to carry my own pregnancy.

Disappointing? Absolutely! Heart wrenching? No doubt! Embarrassing? Indeed! It took me years to even speak the words infertility and miscarriage! However, holding fast to His promise, through my *Faith INfertility* journey, I finally arrived at a place where I was able to release all efforts to even try getting pregnant and just enjoy life as it was. Basking in God's goodness and the love that surrounded me, I clearly remembered as my husband and I celebrated our 10th wedding anniversary, that I told him if God had not blessed me any more than He had already, I was blessed more than enough. My secret to reaching this state was through a combination of the actions described in this book. I was finally still and settled fully IN His peace. My 10th wedding anniversary was in 2011. And yes, in His time, in His way, God directed me, at the beginning of 2012 to execute His wild mysterious plan of purchasing baby blankets when I was not even pregnant. Within less than a year, at the end of 2012, we saw His gift of life in baby Jasmine wrapped in those blankets.

In 2012, my *Faith INfertility* journey was realized. The words, dates, and time were written in my journal a year earlier as directed by God and shared in this book. It happened and God alone receives the glory! My beautiful daughter Jasmine was born through my *Faith INfertility* AND the assistance of IVF. This was after many years of trying to conceive using so many methods including IVF and even being told my only option left was surrogacy. We had been married for over a decade, before our wait to hold our baby was over! For some other moms, it's longer, for others much shorter. For some, it occurs naturally, for others it occurs with the help of fertility treatment.

And if that was not enough, two years later, God doubly blessed me with twin boys. God had restored all the enemy had stolen from me on the first half of this journey. The other half has now been told. **God restores!** Now it's your time to boldly declare:

> *"God, the one and only— I'll wait as long as he says. Everything I need comes from him, so why not? He is a solid rock under my feet, breathing room for my soul, an impregnable castle: I'm set for life," Psalm 62:1-2 (MSG).*

Wherever you are on the journey to becoming a parent, allow yourself to remain in God's presence, and activate your *Faith INfertility*, trusting God to do it His way and in His time. Knowing that His way and His time may be nothing like you had envisioned. But knowing that IN His way and IN His time, when it's executed IN your life, it would be done with perfection. There is no need to hide behind the veil of infertility or the sorrow of an explained or unexplained miscarriage or infant loss. You are not alone and you are not forgotten! God is with you always and will never leave you or forsake you.

Do not allow the secrets of infertility to keep you in the basement of despair. Infertility is just a waiting room before your entrance to a celebration of new life at a specified time, defined by God ,just for you. On our Christian journey, God sometimes allows us to enter into waiting rooms. There, He alone is able to be seen and receive the credit when He opens the entrance door to our overflowing blessings. God is preparing you for the door to be opened. **It's time to walk INfaith, believe INfertility, and jump INfavor** of what

God has for you just outside your waiting room. Activate your faith while in the waiting room, knowing and believing that **God makes ALL things beautiful in His time.**

Have *Faith INfertility*!

"He has made everything beautiful in its time ..." Ecclesiastes 3:11 (NIV).

"Now faith is confidence in what we hope for and assurance about what we do not see," Hebrews 11:1(NIV).

The Stuart Family in our 20ᵗʰ anniversary family photo. This is the evidence of our *Faith INfertility*. Photo credit: Dearean D. Romer

REFERENCES

Maxwell, J. C. (2011). *Put Your Dream to the Test: 10 Questions that Will Help You See It and Seize It.* Thomas Nelson Inc.

Meyers, J. (2012). *Trusting God Day By Day (First Edition).* FaithWords.

White, E. G. (1911). *The Acts of the Apostles.* Mountain View, CA: Pacific Press Publishing Association.

"And now I have it all—and keep getting more! The gifts you sent with Epaphroditus were more than enough, like a sweet-smelling sacrifice roasting on the altar, filling the air with fragrance, pleasing God to no end. You can be sure that God will take care of everything you need, His generosity exceeding even yours in the glory that pours from Jesus. Our God and Father abounds in glory that just pours out into eternity. Yes."

Philippians 4:18-20 (MSG)

CONNECT WITH DOCTORTAZZ

Instagram: @DoctorTazz
Website: www.DoctorTazz.com

For speaking events, webinars, and interviews, book directly on DoctorTazz.com.

To receive your free gift with this purchase, scan QR code below:

Doctor
TAZZ
Build Hope and Bring Joy!